How to Succeed in College

Robert DiYanni
Pace University

Allyn and Bacon
Boston • London • Toronto • Sydney • Tokyo • Singapore

Series Editor: Joseph Opiela
Editorial Assistant: Kate Tolini
Production Coordinator: Susan Brown
Editorial-Production Service: Matrix Productions
Cover Administrator: Suzanne Harbison
Composition Buyer: Linda Cox
Manufacturing Buyer: Megan Cochran

Copyright © 1997 by Allyn & Bacon
A Viacom Company
160 Gould Street
Needham Heights, MA 02194
Web address: abacon.com

Library of Congress Cataloging-in-Publication Data

DiYanni, Robert.
  How to succeed in college / Robert DiYanni.
    p. cm.
  Includes index.
  ISBN 0-205-17526-0
  1. College student orientation. 2. Study skills. I. Title.
LB2343.3.D58 1996
378.1'98—dc20   96-10384
                                     CIP

Printed in the United States of America

10 9 8 7 6 5 4 3 2 1   01 00 99 98 97

For Tina,
whose college experience
was simply incomparable

Contents

Preface

This book can change your life.

Graduating from college can give you an advantage in life. It can provide you with a higher standard of living than you would be likely to attain without earning a degree. *How to Succeed in College* can help you complete your college degree successfully.

This book can also help you to succeed in your college courses. When you apply for a job after graduation, you will be asked to send your college transcript. You will feel better, and you will make a stronger impression on an employer, if your college grades are good. *How to Succeed in College* can help you achieve good grades in your college courses.

It can help you in other ways as well.

If you follow the advice the book offers, you will derive more benefit from your studies. You will enjoy them more. And you will come away from your college experience a more confident, more competent, and more knowledgeable person than when you started.

How to Succeed in College can help you acquire that confidence, competence, and knowledge. It can also help you maximize your potential for learning. The advice you will find here is grounded in the realities of college life. The book's suggestions for successful academic achievement derive from a quarter-century of teaching and advising experience. And its strategies for learning are down to earth and practical.

How is the book organized? What are its educational aims? And what specific kinds of help does it provide?

To help you become an educated person, *How to Succeed in College* provides clear-cut, no-nonsense discussions that describe what you need to know to get the most from your college education. Practical advice about grades, syllabi, courses, and graduation requirements is presented in the context of acquiring a solid education.

The book stresses academic concerns. It can help you understand how to make the college system work for you by focusing on a spectrum of academic matters: planning a course of study, working with professors, improving performance on tests and assignments, developing study and notetaking skills, and learning to manage time effectively.

How To Succeed in College promotes genuine learning and encourages a liberating approach to education. It aims to help you think for yourself, to evaluate critically what you learn in your college courses. It explains how college learning differs from high school education. It identifies the expectations college professors have, and it shows you how you can exceed those expectations.

Focusing on practical methods to improve your academic performance, the book encourages you to develop habits of mind conducive to success in college and beyond. Related aspects of college life, such as the nature of professors and university resources, cocurricular activities, volunteer work, clubs, and student organizations are also examined.

A recurrent theme throughout the book is planning ahead. Careful planning in advance for courses you expect to take and program requirements you need to fulfill can save you grief and aggravation. The importance of acquiring effective academic habits and developing an open, inquiring mind is also emphasized.

How to Succeed in College invites you to think seriously about why you decided to attend college and what you will do there. It urges you to consider carefully how to achieve the best academic return on your investment of time, energy, and money. The book invites you to think not only about what you expect from your college experience but what you want from life as well. It asks you, in short, to develop a set of goals, to consider why you have established them and how you can best go about achieving them.

Two assumptions govern the book's approach. The first is that education is valuable in and of itself, that it is more than a means to an end. Learning is considered worth pursuing for its own sake as well as for what it can help you acquire. The second is that a strong education is your best preparation for living and working in a complex and changing world.

The book is divided into three major parts. Part I concerns getting oriented academically—adjusting to college work, learning how to manage your time, and making the most of your courses. It also includes information and advice about working with instructors and becoming familiar with your college or university's academic and support services.

Part II provides tools for developing confidence and competence in reading with understanding, taking tests and examinations, and improving study and notetaking skills. It also invites you to become a creative thinker and introduces you to the resources and organization of a university library.

Part III provides advice about choosing a major and planning a carefully organized course of study. It concludes with a discussion of the value of literacy, especially cultural literacy.

Each chapter begins with a set of Chapter Highlights that surveys that chapter's topics. A group of Key Questions follows, inviting you to begin thinking immediately about the chapter's central concerns. Numerous topic headings make subjects easy to locate. Three kinds of activities appear throughout the book: (1) Taking Stock sections, which invite self-assessment; (2) Using Your Imagination sections, which encourage speculative thinking; and (3) Exercises, which provide opportunities to implement what you have learned.

These elements encourage you to interact with the book rather than to read it passively. As you read, you are encouraged to think, write, talk, and listen critically, ensuring that you will actively benefit from the practical lessons the book teaches. The more actively you respond to the book's advice and the more you apply its suggestions, the more successful your academic experience in college will be.

Acknowledgments

A number of thoughtful reviewers deserve thanks for reading various drafts of my manuscript with uncanny percipience and making astute recommendations for its improvement. Thanks to Richard E. Lake, Florissant Valley Community College; Jayne Nightengale, Rhode Island College; Susan L. Neste, University of North Dakota; Patricia Hughes, West Georgia College; and Gary Ayers, Lewis and Clark College. My students and colleagues at Pace University require thanks for supporting my efforts and for inviting my participation in our University 101 course. And a special note of thanks to my wife and children, who encouraged my efforts with their questions and their loving support.

Getting Oriented Academically

Chapter *1*

Making the Academic Adjustment to College

Chapter Highlights

The first half of this chapter explains how college differs from high school and why it's important to understand these differences. The second half considers what academic success means to you. It also explains how the college system works. The following topics are discussed:

- Comparisons between high school and college
- The purpose of college
- Academic demands of college courses
- College as a system of requirements and resources
- Grades as a measure of academic success

Key Questions

Take a few minutes to jot down answers to the following key questions:

1. Why have you come to college? What do you want from the experience?
2. What are the requirements for the degree you hope to obtain?
3. What general education requirements exist in your college?
4. What courses are required for a major you are considering?
5. How important are grades to you? Why?
6. What academic rewards would you like to obtain?

From High School to College

Regardless of where you attended high school, you were enrolled in classes with people you knew, taught by teachers who knew you, in classes that were most likely smaller than some of your college classes. In high school you were recognized as an individual with distinctive qualities, skills, and needs. More likely than not, you found your social and academic niches. And perhaps you had friends in an after-school club, sport, or other extracurricular activity. In college you will, of course, make new friends. You will make friends in your different classes. You will have your social friends and perhaps residence hall friends or new friends you make in extracurricular activities. You can help one another adjust to college life's demands.

You can participate in many of the same kinds of extracurricular activities you enjoyed in high school. In fact, choosing such activities carefully and participating in them sensibly will affect your academic performance. Joining a debate team or a chemistry club may enhance your skills in public speaking or extend your knowledge of chemistry. Participating in intramural sports may provide a necessary change of pace from study and work. Perhaps even more important, joining a team or club bonds you with your school, enhancing your satisfaction in being a student there.

Increased Personal Responsibility

In college you will be more academically independent than you were in high school. This increase in independence and responsibility is the most important difference between high school and college. You will be responsible for making decisions for yourself and for monitoring your own academic performance. In class you will have to ask questions. Outside class you will have to do the assigned reading and complete the required assignments.

Academic freedom can be exhilarating. After all, you may say to yourself, "I'm an adult now. I can handle my academic program. I'm a responsible person, and I know where I can get academic help when I need it." And to some extent, you are right to think this way. But you should also be aware that it's easy to become complacent, easy to deceive yourself about what you think you are learning in a course. And it is even easier to fool yourself about how much you can cram into a few weeks of intense study at midterm and final exam time. Too many students have learned—sometimes painfully—that cramming doesn't promote real learning, and that sustained study during the term prepares them much better for academic success.

In college you have more freedom to plan your study time. You have more responsibility and fewer tests and checkpoints than in high school. To achieve academic success, you must handle this freedom wisely. Although other differences between high school and college exist, increased responsibility for your work is the most significant academic difference and the most important for your academic success.

An Increased Workload

Besides the increased academic freedom the college classroom provides, you can expect an increased workload. In a high school English class, for example, you may have spent a month reading *Pride and Prejudice* or *Romeo and Juliet*. In college you will typically have a week to read the novel or the play. An introductory college literature course often includes two or three novels, a couple of dozen stories, three or four plays, and numerous poems. You will be assigned required reading; you may also be expected to write reaction papers, analyses of the works, and perhaps a research paper as well. And though some assigned reading will not be covered in class, you should expect to be tested on it.

And that's only one course. If you are a full-time student, you will be taking from four to six courses at the same time. Each of these courses has its own reading and writing requirements, which in many cases will greatly exceed what was expected of you in high school. If you are a part-time student, you may also have a job that occupies you for many hours per week. Do not expect an instructor in one course to be receptive to your explanation that you couldn't complete an assignment because of work you were doing for other courses, because you have a job, or because your friend was ill. Many instructors feel that their courses deserve priority over your commitments to employers, other courses, or other responsibilities.

You can expect to read longer books and to write longer papers, often in less time than you were given in high school. Fewer tests are spaced at wider intervals, perhaps only two or three times a semester. As a result, you will be responsible for learning and organizing much more information. A careful study plan followed consistently will keep you abreast of assignments and will help you avoid falling behind.

Fewer Class Meetings and Heavier Student Responsibilities

In high school your teachers met you four or five times a week, very likely in classes of anywhere from fifteen to forty students. They saw you in class day in and day out for ten months of the year. Compare that with a college course that meets perhaps twice a week for 75 minutes per session over ten to fifteen weeks. The number of college class meetings in a course approximate one or two month's meetings with a high school instructor. Not surprisingly, under these circumstances your college instructors will probably not know you as well as your high school teachers do.

You should know, too, that some of your instructors may be teaching multiple sections of a course or they may be teaching a variety of other courses, some with large enrollments. If they have many students, they cannot give you the same attention you received in high school. You can compensate by interacting with teaching assistants assigned to smaller discussion sections of large lecture classes. You can also meet with your instructors immediately after class and during their scheduled office hours.

Some college teachers believe that students should be given the freedom to exercise their developing sense of responsibility. These instructors may think it unnecessary to check up on whether students do assigned reading, work progressively on term projects, or understand every aspect of their lectures and assignments. Although some college teachers will give frequent quizzes and will assign numerous short papers and exercises, many will not. In some courses you may experience little pressure to perform until a quarterly test or a midterm exam. In such cases you will be responsible for keeping up with the coursework. No one will be looking over your shoulder; no one will be there to confirm that you are doing your work as you should.

Contact with Instructors

A major difference between high school and college is the type of contact you have with instructors. Some of your college instructors will get to know you. These instructors believe that it's important to know some things about their students' lives and interests beyond the immediate concerns of the particular courses they teach. The degree of personal contact and how this contact is initiated will vary with the instructor. If you want your teachers to get to know you, then you may have to take the initiative yourself since some instructors make more of an effort to know their students than others.

If you attend a large university, you may be enrolled in some courses where students are identified by number rather than by name. In such cases, you can expect to experience some degree of anonymity. To reduce that sense

---

Taking Stock

What is the longest book you read in high school? How much time did you take to read it? What was the most difficult or challenging book you've ever read? Why? From what you can tell from your syllabi and from talking with your instructors and fellow students, what do you think will be the most difficult reading you will do this term? What do you think accounts for its potential difficulty?

Taking Stock

What is your initial impression of your instructors? Of your fellow students? Of your courses?

---

of being lost in a crowd, you will have to establish contact with your instructors, talk with them after class, and make appointments to see them in their offices to discuss topics raised in class. In those cases, the responsibility for approaching your instructors will be yours. In small classes, you will very likely find that instructors take this responsibility upon themselves.

Reasons for Attending College

What are your basic academic goals? You may be in college to earn a degree, to become better educated, to become certified for a particular job, to make more money than you would with a high school degree, and/or to enhance your lifelong experience of learning. Perhaps you wish to change fields of employment or to upgrade your job. Although these goals are related, they differ considerably. You can attend college for any number of years and earn a degree without becoming educated. Conversely, you can become well educated without earning a degree. One is not a necessary by-product of the other. You may wish to think of earning a degree as the practical and immediate outcome of your college and university experience. Acquiring an education is an important and satisfying achievement in itself.

These twin aspects of your college experience should intertwine. Try to see these goals as complementary rather than conflicting. One purpose of this book is to explain how you can integrate the practical demands of earning a degree with the more generalized goal of acquiring an education.

Let's begin by considering some fundamental questions.

Taking Stock

Identify your reasons for being in college. Explain what you hope to derive from your college experience.

Discuss these questions with two of your classmates or friends. Why are they in college and what are their goals? Do the responses from your friends vary? To what extent do they respond as you do? Why?

The Purpose of College

Now that you have done some preliminary thinking about your reasons for attending college, consider some general but basic questions.

First: What do you believe a college education is for?

The obvious answer is that you have come to college to earn a degree—the piece of paper that certifies you as employable by various American and international businesses, educational institutions, public bureaucracies, and private enterprises. According to this view, the degree is necessary not to demonstrate your understanding or capabilities, but to separate those who acquire a credential from those who have not.

This is a simplistic and dangerous perspective. For although a college degree is required for many jobs (in most situations you can't even get an interview without one), a degree is not enough. Employers today are looking beyond the degree to ask what a college graduate can *do*. What these employers have in mind involves these six abilities:

- An ability to apply booklearning to practical situations
- An ability to understand
- An ability to communicate
- An ability to analyze information and solve problems
- An ability to work with others
- An ability to continue learning on the job

Another way of answering the question, "What's a college education for?" is to think not just of immediate prospects but of the long-term gratification an education can provide. Notice that I said "an education" rather than "a degree." You may hope and even expect that a degree will enable you to earn more money than you may earn without one, although there is no guarantee that it will. And you may also hope that a degree may lead to a job that satisfies you intellectually and emotionally as well as financially—though there can be no guarantees about these outcomes, either.

What, then, can an education provide?

Acquiring an education can enhance your self-esteem, perhaps even more than simply earning your degree will. To the extent that the degree represents effort and achievement, a college degree can give you the satisfaction of acquiring knowledge and developing new skills. You will experience the satisfaction of making progress toward a goal.

Many studies have shown that college graduates not only earn more than their less well-educated counterparts, they also have better opportunities for social advancement, longer life expectancies, and generally more fulfilling lives. Education provides the means that can change the way you think,

Taking Stock

Think for a few minutes of what success in college means to you. You might begin by thinking about two or three successful experiences you had in high school. Consider their common features.

process information, and perceive the world. Education can also open doors and provide opportunities not available without it.

College as a System

College is a system with its own set of rules and requirements, its own culture and conventions. This system includes the following general areas:

- Courses and credits
- General education requirements and the major
- Grades and degree requirements

Let's consider these areas briefly one at a time.

Courses and Credits

The basic requirement for earning a college degree is to complete the number of credits needed to graduate. Some of these courses may be prescribed (required courses), while you will select others (electives). Still other courses may be necessary as prerequisites for more advanced ones.

One of the most important things you can do is to read carefully the course catalogue published by your college or university. Be sure you understand the requirements of your degree program, especially the regulations governing its sequence of courses. Make sure you understand your school's policies on adding or dropping courses, class attendance and absence, grades, and deadlines as well as general academic policies governing first-year students. If you don't understand a policy, consult an instructor, counselor, or academic advisor.

Exercise 1-1

Refer to your college bulletin or catalogue to determine the course sequence and how many credits you need to graduate with the type of degree you want. Find out whether there are any other requirements for the degree.

General Education Requirements and the Major

Most universities require all students to take a year or two of general education requirements that range across a broad spectrum of academic disciplines. A university develops a core curriculum or a collection of distribution requirements to ensure that all students are introduced to a broad range of academic disciplines, partly to encourage students to widen their intellectual horizons. The required courses also provide students undecided about a major the chance to explore a range of subjects, at least one of which may be studied further.

Core requirements may be required before you can select courses in your major, or they may be dispersed throughout your college program. Whether you are planning for a career in business or teaching, for example, and whether your major is accounting or history, you will probably need to complete either a specific core curriculum or a set of distribution requirements.

Educators generally agree that students should study something in addition to their area of specialization. They believe it is important for students to develop a broad base of knowledge to complement their area of expertise. They argue that you should learn both a lot about a little (your major field) and a little about a lot (other areas of general knowledge). The required courses provide the academic foundation and the skills to prepare you for the rigors of the more advanced and specialized work in your major. Studies show that within a few years of graduation the majority of college graduates are working in an area other than their college major. The broadening of perspective provided by your general education courses may become useful sooner than you anticipate. In any event, try to see the core curriculum or distribution requirements as opportunities to develop your academic skills and expand your intellectual horizons.

Exercise 1-2

List the requirements for a degree program that interests you. Select one even if you are not sure about your major. Consult your college bulletin or catalogue to see what kinds of core curriculum requirements appear for that program. Identify the kinds of courses you need to meet core requirements—if they apply in your case.

Exercise 1-3

Develop a rough timechart for completing the program on either a part-time or a full-time basis.

How Important Are Grades?

Are you an A student or a B student? Are you an average student or an honor student? Do your grades vary significantly from one subject to another? Do your grades depend on whether a teacher tells you exactly what to do or leaves you pretty much on your own? How do you expect your college grades to compare with your high school grades? How do your parents feel about your grades? How do you feel about your parents' reactions to your grades, and how do you feel about your grades themselves?

One measure of academic success has always been grades. Making good grades is a badge of effort, a sign of achievement. Yet important as grades are, they are not everything. You know that grades do not always accurately reflect how hard you work or how much you learn. You've probably felt better about some B's or even C's you earned in difficult but interesting courses than you have about A's in easier courses, where you may have learned little. It's nice to have the A on your transcript, but having the grade mean something, represent achievement grounded in real understanding, should be more important.

Of course, you should try to get the best grades you can. And you should certainly receive the grades you deserve. Be aware, however, that getting an A in a course may require more than simply performing well on quizzes or exams. There may be other requirements, such as attendance, class participation, and written work, some of which may be quantifiable and some of which may be evaluated more subjectively. Instructors should present this information in the course syllabus and explain how grades are computed and weighted. If these procedures are not explained, ask.

Exercise 1-4

Think back over the most rewarding courses you took in high school. To what extent was your pleasure in those classes and courses determined or affected by grades? Whether or not they gave you much pleasure, what additional factors may have made these courses rewarding?

Your Grade Point Average (GPA)

Your GPA or grade point average is an important index of your academic success. Just because you pass all your courses does not mean that you are performing adequately in college. To remain in school, you need to achieve a satisfactory GPA. Consult your school bulletin or catalogue for details. Generally, however, you need to maintain a 2.00 or C average to remain in good standing academically.

If you transfer to another school after a term or a year of study, only those courses for which you have achieved a grade of C or better will transfer. And even though your current school will give you credit toward your degree for a course you barely passed with a C– or a D, you will not be able to transfer course credits for courses in which you earn such low grades.

Academic Probation

Your school will also have a policy on academic probation, which is designed to identify students who show substandard performance for a term or two but who may be allowed to continue if they can improve their grades. In most schools a committee meets every term to decide the fate of those students on academic probation—usually students whose grades fall below the threshold of a 2.00 average. You should not worry if you do poorly in one or two courses while doing well in most of your others. But if you find yourself getting low grades in many courses, you should seek help immediately from your teachers, your advisor, and any available academic counselor in your school or department.

The W and INC Grades

On occasion it may be in your best interest academically to withdraw from a course with a W grade. When you are permitted to take a W or withdrawal grade, you receive no academic credit for the course, and you may, in fact, still be liable for its tuition. Most schools have a sliding tuition policy, so that if you withdraw within the first two weeks you pay nothing for the course. The longer you wait, however, the more you pay.

You may also find yourself at some time wanting to take an INC or Incomplete in a course. Your school will have a carefully constructed policy on the allowance of Incompletes. Usually a student must have a good reason—financial, medical, or other, to request the privilege of an Incomplete. Some schools require written contracts between teacher and student before the administration will approve an Incomplete. In addition, in many schools you usually have a specified time period (often one term) in which to complete the course work and receive your instructor's grade. In cases where work is not completed on schedule, a grade of F is automatically recorded.

Calculating Your GPA

As you might expect, neither an INC nor an F grade will help your overall grade point average. An INC grade is not averaged in at all. An F is averaged

Letter grades	Meaning	Number grades	GPA values	
			System 1	System 2
A	Excellent	96–100	4.00	4.00
A–		90–95	4.00	3.70
B+	Good	87–89	3.00	3.30
B		84–86	3.00	3.00
B–		80–83	3.00	2.70
C+	Satisfactory	77–79	2.00	2.30
C		74–76	2.00	2.00
C–		70–73	2.00	1.70
D+	Passing	67–69	1.00	1.30
D		64–66	1.00	1.00
D–		60–63	1.00	0.70
F	Failing	0–59	0.00	0.00

in as 0.00 points, while being counted for the number of credits the course carries.

To calculate your GPA, you convert your letter grades to numbers. These numbers are stipulated by your university. In most schools an A = 4.00, a B = 3.00, a C = 2.00, a D = 1.00 and an F = 0.00. Schools calculate pluses (+) and minuses (–) differently. Common practice is for grades to correspond to one of two frequently used systems. Look at the accompanying chart, which explains how these systems relate number grades with their letter counterparts and GPA values.

Final Course Grades

Besides your GPA, your other important grade concern is the final grade you will receive in each of your courses. Be sure that you understand how each instructor computes the final grade. Ask, if it's not clear, how much weight is assigned to each of the following: written assignments, class participation, quizzes and tests, midterm and final examinations, and any special projects.

Instructors may grade you during the course with letter grades and report a final number grade at the end. Or they may grade you with a numerical system that is converted to a letter system for final reported grades.

Some instructors assign extra-credit projects and assignments for students who must raise their grades. Other instructors provide such optional extra-credit grade-enhancing projects and assignments for all students who wish to take advantage of them. And some instructors may weigh some aspects of the coursework—written or oral or tests—much more heavily than other aspects.

It is your responsibility to know, in every instance, how each of your instructors weighs the various components of the course requirements to compute your final grade.

Chapter 2

Managing Your Time

Chapter Highlights

Learning to manage your time, especially to use it productively, is essential for academic success. Time, however, is not always easy to manage or control. You probably have heard yourself say now and then that you do not know where your time goes.

One purpose of this chapter is to make you aware of how you spend your time. Another is to help you use your time efficiently. Chapter topics include the following:

- Assessing how you use your time
- Learning to find extra time
- Managing your time with schedules and lists
- Avoiding wasted time
- Developing strategies to use your time well

Key Questions

1. What major responsibilities take up your time?
2. What things do you need (or would you like) more time for?
3. What things would you like to spend less time doing?
4. Do you think you waste any time? How?
5. How can you begin to make better use of your time to achieve your academic goals?

Thinking about Time

Consider the language we use to talk about time. We *spend* time, *save* it, *use* it, and *waste* it. Spending and saving, of course, imply that time is money, perhaps even that it can be *borrowed* and *lent* as well as saved and spent. Time spent suggests that time is a commodity that gets used up, sometimes used productively and sometimes not.

Even though we can't see time any more than we can see the air, we know it exists by the ways we measure it—in calendar years and months; in days, hours, and minutes; in weeks and weekends; in work time and free time; in deadlines and schedules and timeframes.

We all share the experience of living in time. Our age, race, gender, religion, socioeconomic background, and political or other orientation does not alter the fact that for each of us 60 minutes makes an hour, 24 hours a day, 168 hours a week, and a lifetime a lifetime. We each have been given time to use—our time. We can think of it as a possession, a commodity, a treasure, a gift. But whatever the metaphors we use to think about time and whatever our attitude toward it, we know one thing for sure: our time is limited. That is a simple fact of life.

Using Your Imagination

Think of some other ways of describing time—some other things we compare it to, implicitly or explicitly. You might think about what we "do" with time or what time does to us.

What we do with time _____

_____

What time does to us _____

_____

Assessing How You Use Your Time

Even though all people share the dimension of time, not all people see time the same way or use it in the same ways. Some people take control of time; others remain at its mercy. Since time can't be replaced or made up, it's critical that you use your time well—and productively. The goal of this chapter is to enable you to gain more control of the time you have.

Taking Stock

Think about how you spent your last hour, your last morning, afternoon, evening—yesterday or the day before. Consider how much time you devoted to working, attending classes, studying, eating and sleeping, talking, watching TV, reading, doing chores. Note how much time you cannot account for.

Exercise 2-1

Estimate how much time you will spend doing things such as those mentioned in the previous Taking Stock section. Make an estimate for a full day. Then check yourself by seeing how much time you actually spend doing each of those things tomorrow. To what extent does the day of the week determine what you do with your time?

Exercise 2-2

Keep track of your activities for a week. You can begin by using the accompanying pair of grids to map out how you spend time for a day and a week. When you finish, evaluate what you discover about how you spent your time. Were there any surprises? Did you spend too much time on any activity? Too little? What might you do to adjust how you spend your time?

Using Time Effectively

From the standpoint of academic success, you should assess how well you are using your time to achieve your academic goals. In considering how you spend your time, ask yourself whether you spend too much time diverting energies from tasks such as preparing assignments, reviewing notes, and studying for tests.

To begin making more productive use of your time, you need to know not only how you have been spending it, but also how you want to use your time more effectively. Your attitude is critical. As with going on a diet or saving money, you have to want to improve the ways you use your time.

If you are like most people, you typically feel good about time well spent and a bit guilty over time wasted. What you consider spending or wasting time will not necessarily be the same activities that your friends, classmates,

One Day

6:00 A.M.

7:00

8:00

9:00

10:00

11:00

12:00 noon

1:00

2:00

3:00

4:00

5:00

6:00

7:00

8:00

9:00

10:00

11:00

12:00 midnight

One Week

Monday

Tuesday

Wednesday

Thursday

Friday

Saturday

Sunday

---

or family put in this category. It is important, however, that you be clear in your own mind about what things are important to you and how you can find time to devote to them.

Exercise 2-3

List three activities you consider to be ways of spending your time well. Write a sentence for each explaining why these are useful ways to use your time. What might be some alternative ways of using your time productively?

Productive uses of time:

   1.
   2.
   3.

List three activities you consider taking time away from your studies or other goals. Explain why. What might be better alternative uses of your time?

Unproductive uses of time:

   1.
   2.
   3.

Changing Your Attitude toward Time

Remember that everything begins with your desire to use your time productively and in line with your priorities. Your attitude is crucial. If you spend too much time watching television, for example, you need to decide just how much you will cut down. Make a list of your viewing priorities. Ask yourself some questions. Must you watch late night movies or sit-coms every night? Football games on Sunday afternoons? Rank the kinds of viewing you care most about, and cut back on the less important kinds. Also ask yourself why you may be watching too much television. Are you bored or restless? Are you watching to escape from your responsibilities? To be with friends?

An alternative to cutting back on the amount of television you watch is to modify the kinds of shows you view. You may wish to watch some programs that tie in with courses you are taking, books you are reading, or other intellectual interests you may have. Some of your TV viewing can be used to enhance your understanding of course material or to suggest an approach to an assignment. Use the TV viewing you do have time for to enhance rather than compete with your academic study.

Along with watching television and other leisure activities, you may also have to work or juggle other family responsibilities. In such circumstances, you may experience difficulty in making time for both the things you have to do and the things you most enjoy doing. To help you get through such difficulties, try to remember why you came to college. Remind yourself of your goals and what is required to achieve them. Realize, too, that periods in your life when your free time seems minimal (or perhaps even nonexistent) will eventually end. Look forward to an upcoming vacation when your parents can help with the children, when you have a few days off from work, when you get some relief from the most intense of your time pressures.

Developing Strategies to Use Your Time Productively

You can employ a number of strategies to conserve time and use it efficiently. These include **setting limits** on how much time you allocate for different activities, **avoiding situations** that tempt you to waste time, and **filling dead time,** such as the time you spend waiting in lines, sitting in offices, idling between classes, or waiting for friends or family. (Using such dead time productively brings it back to life.)

On days when you run errands, for example, you can carry a book or index cards with notes to study while you wait in the supermarket, in the lunch line, at the cleaners, in the dentist's office, and so on. On days when you have classes, you can use the time waiting between classes to review your notes, skim passages you previously marked in your text, or think of some questions you'd like to ask in class. Longer stretches of time between classes can be spent in the library or computer lab.

You can also use the times when you are otherwise occupied to better advantage. For example, if you ride a bus, subway, or train, you can probably read or study as you travel. If you set your hair, you can listen to a tape of a book. Some students have hung bulletin boards on bathroom walls or kitchen appliances to review formulas, vocabulary, or notes. One student taped her index cards near the kitchen sink to review while doing dishes. And for times when you eat alone, you can also read or study.

If you find it uncongenial to study under these conditions, you may prefer to substitute activities you find more pleasurable, such as listening to music.

Exercise 2-4

Identify at least one type of dead time in your day, and list three ways to use it more productively.

Dead time _____

Three ways to use it productively:

1. _____

2. _____

3. _____

Taking Stock

Record the amount of time you spend preparing for each of your courses. Include time you spend in class, doing reading and writing assignments, lab and field-work. Include the time you study for quizzes and tests.

Identify any patterns you find in how you spend your time. See if there is a pattern to the way you allocate the time you devote to each of your courses.

Using Your Imagination

Imagine that your days have an extra half-hour period you could use to do anything you wanted. What would you do with the extra time? Why? How might using this extra time help you achieve your goals?

Scheduling Your Time

The most important way to gain control over time is to set up a schedule. Arranging a master schedule of everything you do will help you see just how you spend your time. It will also help you see where you can be flexible about your use of time and where you have to adjust to fixed routines, such as an evening job or child care responsibilities.

You can develop schedules for different purposes and different stretches of time. You can create a quarter-term or semester schedule based on your school's academic calendar and the syllabi for each of your courses. You can make a monthly schedule using an ordinary calendar. And you can make weekly and daily schedules, blocking out chunks of time for your activities and responsibilities. (See Exercise 2-2.)

Exercise 2-5

To create a term schedule, take a sheet of notebook paper and block out major time divisions in the schedule such as midterm and quarter-term points. For a fall semester that begins around Labor Day, for example, the midterm point would fall just after Halloween and the first and third quarter points in late September and late November, respectively. For a ten-week quarterly fall term schedule beginning in late August, your midpoint would be late September and your quarter segments in mid-September and mid-October. Consult your college bulletin or class schedule for exact dates.

Exercise 2-6

From your syllabi, fill in dates for all exams and major tests, including the period allocated for final exams. Next, fill in due dates for all papers and reports. (You may wish to use different colors for exams and papers.) If you have a job or other major form of responsibility—taking care of your children, for example—you should add to your schedule the relevant times, blocking them out with arrows and an identifying label.

Creating a Monthly Calendar

You can get a closer view of your schedule by creating a monthly calendar. For this purpose you can use a calendar of the type found in most bookstores or stationery stores, the type with boxes for each day of the month. You may prefer to create your monthly schedule on a computer or a personal database, such as Wizard.

A monthly calendar lets you see a substantial chunk of time at a glance. By filling in the boxes for the dates of important obligations—work project starting and ending dates, trips planned, exams to be taken and papers due—you can gain a quick sense of what lies ahead for you. You will see easily where your heaviest workload falls and where you have more free or flexible time. By looking at the calendar every day, you will remind yourself of which obligations are imminent and which remain a few weeks away.

Besides posting your academic and other due dates on your term and monthly calendars, you should also include events and plans you are looking forward to as well as to your other obligations. Don't overlook noting the dates of special events such as trips, concerts, sporting events, and other pleasurable occasions.

Exercise 2-7

Buy a monthly block-style calendar or create your own. Fill it in with the important things you will be doing. Include leisure activities—attending a football game, going to the movies, attending a concert—as well as major work and academic responsibilities.

Creating Weekly and Daily Schedules

Term schedules and monthly calendars provide a long-range overview of your time. For a closer look at your commitments, you need to create both weekly and daily schedules. These more immediate arrangements of time will help you see what you have to do now or in the immediate future rather than what is on the horizon for later.

Making a Weekly Schedule

Your weekly schedule is a list of the days of the week across the top of a page with the hours listed vertically. To use a weekly schedule, you would list your classes, required work and other obligations, times for eating and traveling, time for reading and study, and time for exercise and recreation.

SUNDAY	MONDAY	TUESDAY	WEDNESDAY	THURSDAY	FRIDAY	SATURDAY
1	2	3	4	5	6	7
8	9	10	11	12	13	14
15	16	17	18	19	20	21
22	23	24	25	26	27	28
29	30	31				

Exercise 2-8

Create a weekly schedule for the next full week. Be sure to include time for all your activities, including recreation. Compare your weekly schedule with those of your classmates.

Making a Daily Schedule

To create a daily schedule, you could use one of the published systems with preprinted sheets like this one. Or you can simply use a small notepad or an index card, which you can put in your purse or pocket.

Exercise 2-9

Make a daily schedule for tomorrow and the next day. You can make a simple list, or you can use the blank sample here. Compare your daily schedules with those of your classmates.

The Problem of Procrastination

Perhaps the most serious problem with time most people confront is procrastination. To procrastinate means to delay—sometimes, in fact, to delay to the point of not doing the thing at all. You procrastinate when you put off doing something till later that you could be (or should be) doing now.

Taking Stock

Consider why you procrastinate. Make a list of things you avoid or put off doing. Beside each one give the reasons for your procrastination.

Activity _____

Reason for Avoiding _____

Activity _____

Reason for Avoiding _____

Activity _____

Reason for Avoiding _____

Days Time	Monday	Tuesday	Wednesday	Thursday	Friday	Saturday	Sunday
7:00							
8:00							
9:00							
10:00							
11:00							
12:00							
1:00							
2:00							
3:00							
4:00							
5:00							
6:00							
7:00							
8:00							
9:00							
10:00							
11:00							

Daily Schedule

6:00 A.M.

7:00

8:00

9:00

10:00

11:00

12:00 noon

1:00

2:00

3:00

4:00

5:00

6:00

7:00

8:00

9:00

10:00

11:00

12:00 midnight

People tend to procrastinate or put off those things they don't enjoy doing or enjoy doing less than they enjoy doing other things. But there are other reasons for procrastination. You may procrastinate because you're afraid of failing at something, or of not doing it well, whether it's taking a test or asking someone for a date. You may procrastinate because you feel depressed or overwhelmed, or because you are disorganized.

Techniques for Avoiding Procrastination

Making and sticking to a schedule—daily, weekly, monthly, or longer—can help reduce a tendency to procrastinate. But you can do other things to avoid procrastination as well. These include breaking large tasks into smaller ones, rewarding yourself for small accomplishments, planning for extra time, taking breaks, and dealing with disturbances.

Break Large Tasks into Smaller Ones

For times when a task seems overwhelming—writing a long report or studying for a final exam—you can use the divide-and-conquer technique. Breaking a large task down into smaller, more manageable parts is a practical and very useful approach. You are more likely to get started if your goal is to settle on a topic for a research paper or compile a list of relevant sources than if you are thinking of completing the entire project.

For example, when you read a book of 1,000 pages, break it down into smaller sections. Fyodor Dostoyevsky's novel *The Brothers Karamazov* is organized in four major parts, each of which has approximately 250 pages. If you are unaccustomed to reading long books, just thinking about reading *The Brothers Karamazov* may be daunting. Instead of regarding Dostoyevsky's novel as a single book, think of it as four small books. You feel more confident about being able to read the first "book" in Dostoyevsky's novel than about reading all 1,000 pages.

In the same way that you can break the big book down into smaller ones, you can break the first small "book" down into sections. In fact, Dostoyevsky has already done this for you by creating chapters. Get started by telling yourself you will read the first chapter or perhaps the first two chapters. Or tell yourself you will read for 15 or 20 minutes. What often happens when you do something like this is that you find yourself reading an additional chapter or reading for 10 or 15 minutes more.

Remember, however, that there's more involved than simply getting started. Start by all means. But then keep going. Take a section at a time. Let your interest and your momentum carry you. Before you know it, you will have read a quarter of the first part, then half, and then all of it. Stop from time to time and calculate how much you've read—how many minutes or hours overall, how many pages. You should enjoy measuring your accomplishment.

Reward Yourself for Completing Tasks

When you decide on a topic for a research paper or compile that list of sources, when you read that first chapter of that novel or study for that 15- or 20-minute period you promised, then reward yourself. Take a walk, eat a favorite snack, watch a favorite TV show, go to the movies, or simply give yourself a break.

Be honest with yourself, though. Don't reward yourself for tasks you complete haphazardly or those you do not complete at all. Instead, evaluate the situation, reassess your goal, and try again. Then, with success, enjoy that reward.

Leave Extra Time

In scheduling time to complete a long or complex project, plan to finish before the deadline. That way, if you run into problems, you have some extra time to finish on schedule. Planning to finish ahead of schedule allows time for various unanticipated distractions, obstacles, and competing obligations. Starting early on projects also helps you gain momentum that can carry you through to the end when you are interrupted by unanticipated distractions.

Allow yourself the flexibility of readjusting your goals for large projects. If you miss a deadline for part of your goal, set up another deadline, but this time be sure to make it. The deadline for the final project will rarely be extended. It's up to you to set smaller deadlines for yourself based on smaller goals. As you complete each of those goals, you will cumulatively be completing the overall project—ideally, according to schedule. Leaving extra time is especially important when you write a paper or report. Don't schedule only enough time to complete an assignment. Leave additional time to set it aside and then revise it.

Taking Stock

Consider the last project you completed on schedule. How did you accomplish the task? Did you leave extra time? Was there flexibility in your schedule? Consider a project you are working on (or supposed to be working on) now. How are you budgeting your time for it? What small-scale goals have you set, and how have you broken the project into smaller segments? According to what plan and schedule?

Exercise 2-10

Think back over times when you needed uninterrupted time to work on a project. What did you do to gain that time? Look ahead to a point this term when you know you will need uninterrupted time to study for a major exam, write a paper, or complete a project. Consider how you will acquire that time.

Two Scenarios

Here are two scenarios.

Scenario 1. It's a Monday evening around 7 P.M. You have difficult math problems and some heavy literature reading due for Tuesday morning. You would like to relax and have some fun before tackling the assignments. If you watch TV or go out with your friends for a couple hours, you may wind up thinking about the work you should be doing. Your pleasure will be tempered by the nagging guilt about the assignments.

Scenario 2. It's Monday at 7 P.M. You decide to tackle the math first, giving it an hour and a quarter. At 8:20 you take a 10-minute break, and at 8:30 you begin reading the literature assignment, which takes you until 9:45. With the work completed for Tuesday morning's classes, you decide to go out for pizza with friends, watch TV, or simply go to bed early to get a fresh start for the next day. Doing your work first permits you to enjoy whatever else you decide to do—free of guilt—without the nagging feeling that you should be doing something else.

Few things are more frustrating than feeling out of control as you struggle to find time to attend classes, study, work, take care of family, socialize, and fulfill other demands on your time. By learning to control time rather than being at its mercy, you will feel better about yourself. Your attitude toward school and studying will improve. And you will experience the rewards of setting up and sticking to a schedule. Your leisure time will be worry free since you will feel confident about allocating time to complete your assignments. You will feel in greater control of your life since you have managed to allocate time for all your activities. And you will enjoy the pleasure of seeing your assignments completed—on time, according to schedule.

Chapter 3

Getting the Most from Your Courses

Chapter Highlights

This chapter stresses the importance of understanding course aims and requirements. It describes various types and levels of courses and explains how to determine course requirements. The chapter focuses on individual courses and can be read in conjunction with Chapter 11, on choosing a major and planning a course of study. Topics covered include:

- Interpreting the course syllabus
- Using the syllabus as a guide to study
- Going beyond course requirements

Key Questions

Take a few minutes to think about the following key questions.

1. What do you expect to get from your college courses?
2. How can you get as much as possible from your courses?
3. How can you demonstrate your desire to excel in your courses?

To get the most from your courses, you should do three things. First, fulfill all course requirements—on schedule. Begin by studying your course syllabi. Second, find ways to learn more by considering your instructor as an educational resource. Third, consider the relationship of each course to other courses you take, whether the other courses are within or outside your prospective major or concentration.

We can begin with basic matters—with the course as an entity in and of itself.

Reading the Syllabus

Your academic responsibility begins with understanding explicit course requirements as stipulated by the syllabus. It continues with understanding the instructor's implicit expectations as reflected between the lines of the syllabus as well as from his or her style, manner, and tone.

Here is a syllabus for a course in American literature. Read it carefully and make sure you understand all that it stipulates. When you have done that, see if you can get a sense of the instructor's further expectations behind the stated requirements.

Exercise 3-1

Analyze the syllabus on p. 31. Make a list of observations about course requirements, course readings, and assignment schedules. Jot down a few questions you have about the syllabus.

Observations

Questions

Dr. Robert DiYanni   Pace University   Spring 1996

Literature 115 (American I)   Dyson College   Choate 213

Texts: Thoreau: <u>Walden</u>; Hawthorne: Stories; Hawthorne: <u>Scarlet</u> <u>Letter</u>; Fanny Fern: <u>Ruth Hall</u>; Poe: Stories; Whitman: <u>Leaves of</u> <u>Grass</u>; Dickinson: <u>Final Harvest</u>; Douglass: <u>The Life</u>; Twain: <u>Adventures of Huckleberry Finn</u>.

Requirements: Faithful attendance with intelligent participation;
two papers, details forthcoming;
passing grades on midterm and final exams.

Schedule:

2/1 — Introduction

2/3 — Thoreau: <u>Walden</u> chs. 1-5

2/8 — Thoreau: <u>Walden</u> chs. 6-12

2/10 — Thoreau: <u>Walden</u> chs. 13 to end

2/15 — Hawthorne: "Young Goodman Brown"
"The Minister's Black Veil"

2/17 — Hawthorne: "Roger Malvin's Burial"
"Rappaccini's Daughter"

2/22 — Hawthorne: <u>Scarlet Letter</u>: Custom House and Chapter 1-2

2/24 — Hawthorne: <u>Scarlet Letter</u>: Chapters 3-12

3/1 — Hawthorne: <u>Scarlet Letter</u>: Chapters 13-16

3/3 — Hawthorne: <u>Scarlet Letter</u>: Chapters 17-24

3/8 — Fern: <u>Ruth Hall</u> (first half)

3/8 — Fern: <u>Ruth Hall</u> (to conclusion)

3/15 and 3/17 — Off (Spring Break)

3/22 — Poe: "The Cask of Amontillado" / "The Black Cat"

3/24 — Poe: "Ligeia" / "The Fall of the House of Usher"

3/29 — Poe: "The Purloined Letter"
"A Descent into the Maelstrom"

3/31 — Midterm Test

Continued

```
DiYanni Continued

4/5  —  Whitman: "When I Heard the Learn'd Astronomer"
                 "The Dalliance of the Eagles"
                 "A Noiseless Patient Spider"
4/7  —  Whitman: "Song of Myself"

4/12 —  Whitman: "There Was a Child Went Forth"
                 "Crossing Brooklyn Ferry"
4/14 —  Whitman: "Cavalry Crossing a Ford"
                 "The Wound Dresser"
                 "Reconciliation" / "A Sight in Camp"
                 "Vigil Strange I Kept" / "Come up . . . Fields"

4/19 —  Dickinson: 199, 241, 249, 324, 341, 435, 449, 465, 480,
                   536, 547
4/21 —  Dickinson: 632, 650, 668, 986, 1072, 1078, 1100, 1129,
                   1138, 1705

4/26 —  Douglass: Life (first half)
4/28 —  Douglass: Life (to conclusion)

5/3  —  Twain: Huck Finn (first half)
5/5  —  Twain: Huck Finn (to conclusion)

5/12 —  Final Exam
```

Comments on the Syllabus

The course requirements seem to be laid out clearly enough. You might want to ask, though, what is meant by "faithful attendance." How many cuts are permitted? Are you penalized for being absent? Do you have the benefit of one cut? Of two or more? Is it necessary to have a written excuse or explanation for an absence? For only those absences beyond the allowed limit? And what about the paper? When will it be due, how long should it be, and what kind of paper is expected?

You might also wonder whether you can expect to be called on in class or whether the instructor will call on only those who volunteer.

These are important considerations. Get in the habit of questioning course requirements so that you understand *exactly* what will be expected of you.

Like other aspects of college life, class attendance involves responsibility. By handling the responsibility of attending class well, you demonstrate your

Taking Stock

What about the sample syllabus's stipulation of "intelligent participation"? Does that mean that your class comments will be evaluated? Or does the instructor mean to suggest that if you are prepared with the reading or writing assignment for the day, pretty much whatever you say will qualify as "intelligent participation"? Can authentic expressions of confusion or questions about the readings be considered a form of "intelligent participation"? Or does the instructor mean to suggest that you need to be ready with some answers?

maturity. Regular attendance in class increases your opportunities to participate in class discussion, respond to your instructor's questions, and ask some of your own. It also helps you identify what kinds of participation your instructor considers especially significant. Your active involvement in the course demonstrates your commitment to it and also shows your instructor how well you have prepared. It's not an accident that there is a high and direct correlation between class attendance and grades. Students who earn the highest grades attend class faithfully.

Exercise 3-2

Consult your school bulletin or catalogue on attendance policy. Is attendance mandatory? Can each instructor set attendance policy? Or is there a departmental, school, or university-wide policy?

Considering Attendance

Some instructors insist that you attend class without fail. They will mark their class lists meticulously, and they may penalize students who exceed a small number of permitted cuts. Other instructors may not be nearly so careful about attendance, nor will they establish a strict policy. This does not mean that they won't care if you miss classes. Most of them will care. They may even interpret your repeated absences as lack of interest in the course and possibly even as a slight to them personally.

Find out what you can about each instructor's attendance policy. Learn to what extent attendance and class participation contribute toward your grade. Attend class regularly, rarely missing, except for emergencies. And finally, if you do miss classes, contact your instructors to let them know why—preferably before class, if possible. Never ask whether you missed anything important. Assume that you have; assume that instructors consider each of their class meetings important. Ask instead about the material discussed and what you can do to make up the missed work, or at least ensure that you understand what was covered in your absence. Besides contacting the instructor, ask a classmate what happened during the class, whether any additional assignments were given, or whether any changes were made in the course schedule.

Taking Stock

List the names, office locations, and hours of each of your instructors. For any you don't know, call the departmental secretary.

Course 1

Instructor _____

Office location _____

Office hours _____

Course 2

Instructor _____

Office location _____

Office hours _____

Course 3

Instructor _____

Office location _____

Office hours _____

Course 4

Instructor _____

Office location _____

Office hours _____

Course 5

Instructor _____

Office location _____

Office hours _____

You don't want to find yourself in the position of returning from a missed class to discover that a quiz that had been announced while you were absent is being given, or that it counts heavily toward your final grade. Also be sure to copy a classmate's notes. (Be aware, however, that another student's notes are no substitute for in-class discussion, even when those notes are complete and accurate, which may not always be the case.)

The Instructor's Name, Office Location, and Hours

Don't overlook the obvious aspects of a syllabus. Note the spelling of the instructor's name. When it comes time to submit a paper, be sure you spell your instructor's name correctly. Notice, too, the location of the instructor's office and his or her office hours. If instructors are careful enough to list these, you can be reasonably sure they will be available during those times. If office location and hours are not given, ask for them, even if your instructor holds no regular hours, and schedules individual meetings by appointment.

Focusing on Exams and Required Written Work

Let's look now at the requirement concerning midterm and final exams. You are within your rights to ask about the nature of the midterm and final tests. At the beginning of a course, instructors often indicate what kind of test to expect at the quarter or midpoint of the course. If they are not specific about their tests, perhaps a general description of those tests can be provided initially, with more specific details given as the test dates approach. It certainly doesn't hurt to ask about these things. You can learn a lot from instructors by how direct and helpful they are in describing the kinds of exams they give. Ask, too, whether samples of old exams are available in the library for review.

Nor should you overlook the sample syllabus requirement concerning the written work for the course: "two papers, details forthcoming." What kind of papers? How long? Are the requirements for both the same? If not, how do they differ? And when will the details be forthcoming? Also: how much weight will papers and exams carry? And to what extent will attendance and class participation be figured into computing class grades?

As specific as instructors may make their syllabi, questions like these can clarify matters. Be particularly attentive to due dates for required reading and writing assignments. Don't be afraid to ask about penalties for being unprepared for class or for being late with a paper. It's better to know from the start that your grade will be lowered for a late paper or that late papers will not be accepted barring medical catastrophe. You don't want to be surprised by such rules far into the term.

Exercise 3-3

Select syllabi for two of your courses and analyze them. First list your observations about texts, requirements, attendance, grading, and the like. Then jot down some questions you would like to ask the instructor to clarify course requirements.

Syllabus for _____

Observations _____

_____

_____

_____

Questions _____

_____

_____

_____

Syllabus for _____

Observations _____

_____

_____

_____

Questions _____

_____

_____

_____

Understanding the Schedule of Assignments

Consider also the schedule of reading and writing assignments the syllabus stipulates. Make sure you understand how the syllabus works. Look, for example, at the sample syllabus listing: "Hawthorne: *Scarlet Letter:* Chapters

3–12." Does this mean that Chapters 3 through 12 (including Chapter 12) are to be read (and thought about) *before* the class discussion on February 24? Or does it mean that the chapters will be introduced that day but can be read later? Check to see whether all the reading assignments are clearly stipulated. Notice, for example, that the Douglass and Twain assignments indicate that the first half of each writer's book is to be read for 4/26 and 5/3, respectively. You may want to ask for a chapter or page number for those reading assignments.

Look also for dates where the reading seems especially heavy. See if there is any section of the syllabus where writing assignments follow one another unusually quickly. Try to gauge the course requirements in terms of the hours you will need to do the work. In short, attend to the *implications* of the syllabus for your daily or weekly study time. Even though an instructor may be reluctant to quantify the number of hours per class or per week that you should be spending on the course, you can gain a reasonably good sense of the course's time requirement by considering the length and frequency of the assignments and by assessing their difficulty. And you should be aware that many instructors consider 2 hours of preparation for 1 hour of class a reasonable proportion of outside work to classwork.

It is important, moreover, to know not only how heavy the overall demands of reading (and writing) may be, but also when those demands become heaviest. Some instructors create syllabi with the heaviest reading demands at the beginning, reasoning that students are freshest and most eager at that point in the course. Other instructors leave the heaviest reading load and often the biggest and most important writing assignments for the end, reasoning that students will then be in a better position to meet their demands. Still other instructors develop course syllabi that build in critical checkpoints at strategic places in the term (quarter, half, three-quarter, final; or one-third, two-thirds, final) spreading out both their own work and yours as well. If the syllabus doesn't specify critical checkpoints, try to establish them yourself by talking to the instructor.

Taking Stock

Look over two of your course syllabi to see where the heaviest assignments fall. Check to see whether you will have exams or papers due on the same day or on consecutive days. Preview all of your syllabi together to check for times you will need to do advanced or extra work for one or another of your courses.

After scanning all your syllabi, compile a list of major assignments with their due dates so you can begin planning a reasonable schedule to complete them.

Reviewing Writing Assignments

In considering the writing assignments, ask whether there is opportunity for revision. Ask whether this opportunity occurs before or after a grade has been assigned. Find out, also, how revised papers are graded—whether the revised grade displaces the original grade or whether the two grades are averaged.

In addition, try to get some sense of what your instructor values in written work. In writing papers, you will, of course, want to present your ideas in a logically organized form, with correct grammar, punctuation, and spelling. But if you make an occasional mistake—or if, in proofreading your paper, you overlook an occasional error—how much will that cost you? Ask as well about your oral work. To what extent, for example, is what you say in class going to be evaluated?

These and other matters can all be discussed in conjunction with the course syllabus—matters such as whether your papers must be typed; whether assignments can be submitted on disk; whether papers should be folded a certain way; whether they should be clipped or stapled or with pages left separate. Successful college work begins with understanding the rules and procedures established by individual instructors in their courses. Since those rules and procedures vary from one course to another and from one instructor to another, you need to question every syllabus and every instructor about your responsibilities and theirs.

Exercise 3-4

List the requirements for written work for each course you are taking.

Course 1 _____

Course 2 _____

Course 3 _____

Course 4 _____

Course 5 _____

Check to see if a single standard prevails throughout a department or school for papers and reports. Identify the conventions of manuscript form. Indicate where you can find your school's policy on plagiarism.

Considering Other Aspects of the Syllabus

Attend to any unusual aspects of the syllabus. If holidays are built into the university calendar, they ought to be observed in an individual instructor's syllabus. If they are not, you should ask why they are not. Conversely, if days off are stipulated on the syllabus that are not officially recognized by the university, you should be aware of them. Perhaps a substitute class may be required to make up the missed class time. Perhaps the instructor feels that isn't necessary. Check your school calendar and your course syllabi carefully. If you notice a discrepancy, call it to the instructor's attention. If something puzzles you, ask. It doesn't hurt to be clear on such matters from the start.

Asking about Grades

Aside from an occasional course you might take Pass/Fail, nearly all of your college courses involve a grade, usually a letter grade from A to F. Besides carefully reading your college bulletin or catalogue on university grading policy, you should also be clear about each instructor's interpretation and application of that policy. You may need to ask your instructors a few questions to clarify their position. In doing so, it is best to avoid giving the impression that your primary interest is your course grade rather than course content. But simply as a point of clarification, you should be able to ascertain how your instructors evaluate your performance and how they weigh each of their course's requirements.

Some instructors lay out their grading procedures in detail, quantifying the value of each quiz, test, project, and examination. Other instructors do this more generally, perhaps by counting tests for a third of your grade, papers for another third, and the final exam for a quarter, with the balance (in this case, 8%) to be made up from class attendance and participation. However detailed an instructor's grading information may be, make sure you understand it, especially the weight allotted to each of its requirements. Be sure that you understand the grading scale for the course. And, finally, make sure you know the procedure for resolving a disputed grade, whether for a paper, lab, report, or test, or for a course.

Going Beyond the Syllabus

The syllabus, however detailed and however carefully explained, is not the course. Although the syllabus provides many clues about the course requirements as well as insight into the temperament and perspective of the instructor, it may not indicate how difficult or advanced the course is. Those things you should be able to determine from the course catalogue, from a conversation with your advisor, and from the grapevine. In addition, you should try to determine how any individual course relates to other courses you may take. You can glean this information from reading the university bulletin or catalogue and through conversations with your advisor and friends. Don't expect this kind of information to be suggested by a course syllabus.

Beyond these specific concerns, you'll also need to see how the course fits into the university curriculum overall. What specific requirement does it fulfill? What, ideally, are its aims and goals? How are these aims or goals to be achieved? What is your role? What is the instructor's role in assuring that the course goals are achieved?

Besides understanding the ideals, goals, and ambitions of the course, you should also try to acquire a realistic sense of its limits. What does it not attempt to do? What are its intellectual boundaries? And to what extent is a given course likely to be transferable to another institution?

Here are a few course descriptions accompanied by brief comments.

HISTORY 112   American Civilization Since 1877   3 credits.

A survey of political, social, and cultural developments in the United States since 1877, emphasizing the Populist and Progressive movements, the New Deal, and the role of the United States in international affairs.

Comment: This is a basic or introductory course. You can project from the description that it will be a survey course that covers a wide span of time and a broad range of topics. In many schools, the low course number may also indicate a basic or preliminary course; in other schools, a 100 number may designate a more advanced course.

HISTORY 298   Historiography and the Historical Process   3 credits.

Open to Honor students and others with a minimum GPA (grade point average) of 3.3. Strongly recommended for history majors.

A workshop/seminar focusing on history as a process. This course features lectures and discussions on the nature of history; techniques of historical research; the role of critical thinking in historical decision making; historiography; and modern trends in the field of history such as computer assisted research, production of documentaries, fictionalized history on film and in print, museums, historical restoration and preservation.

Comment: This is clearly an advanced course, as reflected in its higher number, its title, its topics, its restrictions, and its seminar organization. (In a seminar students assume more responsibility for the actual management of classroom discussion. They also present more in-class papers and do more extensive research than in a typical lecture course.)

HISTORY 280   History of American Women   3 credits.

Social history of American women from colonial times to the present, with emphasis on changes in the political, economic, legal and social position of women. Consideration of the development of feminist ideology.

Comment: This is also an advanced course, though not as advanced as the seminar in historiography. Notice that there are no restrictions or prerequisites, thus making the course available to all students. Its focus on women in American history does not seem to require preliminary basic knowledge of the sort you would get from taking traditional surveys of American history such as History 112 described earlier. Nonetheless, you might feel more comfortable and more confident taking a course like this as a junior or senior rather than as a first- or second-year student. Notice, too, that the course ranges from colonial times to the present and that its focus is on changes in women's status and roles. You might also think about the inclusion of the final comment about feminist ideology. Does this mean that the entire course will be taught from a strongly ideological viewpoint? Or does it suggest that the course will include some attention (minor? major?) to the historical development of feminism? Here is a case where you might benefit from speaking to the instructor before enrolling in the course.

Going Beyond the Course Requirements

In some courses you will be given a contract that stipulates what you need to do to earn a particular grade. To earn a C in a given section of an introductory psychology course, for example, you may be required to miss no more than six class hours and write two lab reports and two papers. To earn a B, you should miss no more than four class hours, write three lab reports and three papers, and submit a journal of your observations about the course. To earn an A, you should miss no more than two class hours, write four papers and lab reports, submit a class journal and also do an additional project of your choice after securing your instructor's approval.

In most courses, however, you will be presented with a syllabus and a set of requirements. If you satisfy the requirements, you should expect to pass the course. Your grade may be determined by how well you satisfy the requirements measured against the performance of others students in the class or against a standard set by the instructor.

But there is more to a course than simply meeting its demands and fulfilling all requirements. If you really want to get the most out of a course, you should look for ways to go beyond the requirements. Your motives for doing more than what's required can be anything from trying to achieve the highest grade to wanting to learn as much as possible about the subject.

Some ways to go beyond the requirements include reading books and articles that the instructor recommends, writing additional papers, and creating your own projects related to the course materials or perspective. You might do research on a problem raised in the course or might write a paper on an issue debated in class. You might write on a book from a list of suggested readings.

Doing any of these things will demonstrate your seriousness. They may also help your grade. More important, however, they will enhance what you learn. Such efforts should also give you additional opportunities to talk with your instructors and learn from them in informal conversations between classes or during their office hours. Going beyond the course requirements in one sense involves going outside the classroom to tap the instructor's and university's resources. As a student paying tuition, you are entitled to make use of those resources. As a lifelong learner, you are developing skills to go beyond the course requirements.

Exercise 3-5

For two courses, think of an extra assignment you might give yourself to help increase your understanding of the material and to show the instructor how serious a student you are.

Course 1

Extra assignment _____

_____

Course 2

Extra assignment _____

_____
_____

Exercise 3-6

Consider how the instructors in each of the two courses described previously can help you improve your performance. Try to set up a meeting with at least these two instructors to find out more about them and to consider ways they can help you learn the subjects they teach. Make a list of things you learned from talking with them.

1. _____

2. _____

3. _____

4. _____

5. _____

6. _____

Besides these traditional ways of going beyond the requirements, you can also use your extra- and cocurricular activities as additional sources of learning. Look for connections between the things you do in your leisure time and what is discussed in your courses. Attending a concert or lecture, participating in a social outreach program, even watching a film or television show can provide you with added ways to make the most of your courses. There may be something in your social and personal life that starts you thinking, something you can relate to your coursework.

If you are a musician, for example, you may also be able to capitalize on your knowledge of music in courses where musical versions of literary or theatrical works have been performed. In a course on the Bible, for example, as a musician you might be able to contribute to the class with your knowledge of music inspired by the Bible, whether that music be something popular such as the Broadway play based on the Genesis story of Joseph (*Joseph and His Amazing Many-Colored Coat*) or the rock opera *Tommy*, based on the New Testament, or a symphonic work such as Camille Saint-Saëns' *The Deluge*, which is based on the biblical account of Noah and the Flood. Other examples of how your enjoyment, knowledge, and experience of music may be useful could materialize in a poetry class or perhaps in an American history course, in which formal or informal study of an aspect of American music (Civil War songs, for example) can be tapped as a way to go beyond the requirements.

The point is simply to use your interests, knowledge, skills, and leisure pursuits to enrich your academic work and ensure that you get the most you can from your courses.

Exercise 3-7

Identify two extra- or cocurricular activities you could participate in that can be related to one or another of your courses. Explain briefly what you might gain from the activity and how it relates to the course(s).

Activity 1 _____

Benefits _____

Activity 2 _____

Benefits _____

_____

_____

_____

Exercise 3-8

Consider the following syllabus, which is more elaborate than the one presented earlier in the chapter. Analyze the syllabus and do the following:

(a) List any questions you have about what is expected of you.
(b) Jot down the key dates when papers are due.
(c) Estimate when reading assignments seem heaviest. (Perhaps add a question about this to your list in [a].)
(d) Explain in a couple of sentences which kind of syllabus you prefer, the
brief syllabus on pp. 31–32 or this one.

  a. Questions _____

_____

  b. Paper dates _____

_____

  c. Heavy reading _____

_____

  d. Preferred syllabus _____

     Reason _____

```
Dr. Michael Gillen     INT 200: The Vietnam Era      Fall 1996
Dr. Robert DiYanni     History and Literature        3 credits


Texts: Young, The Vietnam Wars 1945-1990; Gettleman et al.,
Vietnam and America: A Documented History; Butler, A Good Scent
from a Strange Mountain; Caputo, A Rumor of War; Du, The Tale of
Kieu (excerpts); Emerson, Winners and Losers (excerpts); Green,
The Quiet American; Kovic, Born on the Fourth of July (ex-
cerpts); Herr, Dispatches; Mason, In Country; O'Brien, The
```

Things They Carried; Van Devanter, Home Before Morning (excerpts); miscellaneous poems, songs, and articles.

Requirements: Faithful attendance with prepared and intelligent
participation.

Three written assignments (see options at end of
syllabus).

Midterm and final examinations.

Trip to the Vietnam Veterans Memorial
in Washington.

Dinner at a Vietnamese restaurant in Manhattan.

Tentative Schedule:

Wk I   M —   INTRODUCTION: WHERE, WHAT, WHY?
GEOGRAPHY / EARLY HISTORY
OUR STORIES

W —   EARLY POETRY (handout—packet)
CHINESE INFLUENCE
Young, 319–329 / Documents 1

Wk II   M —   RELIGION AND PHILOSOPHY: CONFUCIANISM,
TAOISM, BUDDHISM (handout—packet)
EARLY HISTORY CONTINUED / ANCESTOR WORSHIP

W —   LATER POETRY / THE TALE OF KIEU / LAMENT OF
A WARRIOR'S WIFE (handout—packet)
THE ROLE OF WOMEN

Wk III M —   WESTERN CONTACT
TRADITION OF RESISTANCE
TAY SON REBELLION / NGUYEN DYNASTY
ARRIVAL OF "Round Eyes" / EARLY FRENCH RULE
Young, ch. 1 / Documents 1, 2

W —   Green: The Quiet American I

Wk IV   M —   Price of Nuoc Mam
The Roots of War and The First Indo-China War
(film excerpts)

Continued

```
Wk IV    M —    HO CHI MINH
                Young, ch. 2 / Documents 3-5
         W —    Green: The Quiet American II


Extra Session: Screening of film Indochine, Time and room to be
                determined


Wk V     M —    WORLD WAR / COLONIAL WAR / KOREA
                FDR / HST / DDE
                Young, chs. 3-4 / Documents 6-13
         W —    LA SALE GUERRE
                Dien Bien Phu / Geneva / SEATO
                IKE / JFK / LBJ


Wk VI    M —    AMERICAN INVOLVEMENT
                American War (film)
                Young, chs. 5-6 / Documents 35-39
                Caputo: A Rumor of War I
         W —    Caputo: A Rumor of War II


Wk VII   M —    IA DRANG
                Young and Brave (film)
         W —    MIDTERM TEST (1 hour in class; + two take-home
                essays)


Wk VIII  M —    PRE-TET
                Herr: Dispatches I
                America's Enemy (film)
                Young, chs. 7-8 / Documents 40-41
         W —    TURNING POINT: TET (1968)
                Herr: Dispatches II
                Tet (film)
                Young, chs. 9-11 / Documents 52-55


Extra Session: Screening of film When Heaven and Earth Changed
                Places
                Handout of book excerpt for discussion
```

```
Wk IX   M —   ROLE OF THE MEDIA
              O'Brien: The Things They Carried I
              Arlen (excerpts)
        W —   THE MEDIA
              O'Brien: The Things They Carried II


Wk X    M —   COMBAT
              Born on the Fourth of July (film, excerpts)
              84 Charlie Mopic (film)
        W —   MY LAI: MORAL AND LEGAL QUESTIONS
              My Lai (film)
              Young, ch. 12 / Document 56



Extra Session:  Clips: Platoon / Coming Home / Deer Hunter
              Apocalypse Now / Full Metal Jacket
              Born on the Fourth of July



Wk XI   M —   THE ANTI-WAR MOVEMENT / Protest songs and poems
              Only the Beginning / The War at Home
                 (film excerpts)
              Young, ch. 10 / Documents 42-51, 62
        W —   THE ANTI-WAR MOVEMENT
              Hearts and Minds (film)


Wk XII  M —   WOMEN AND WAR
              Van Devanter (excerpts) / Nurses (article)
              Front Line piece on Women and the War
              Mason: In Country I
              Young: ch. 13
        W —   Mason: In Country II


Wk XIII M —   THE END OF THE WAR
              The Wall: The Vietnam Veterans War Memorial
              Butler: A Good Scent from a Strange Mountain
              Young: ch. 14 / Documents 57-63, 65-68
```

Continued

Wk XIII W —   LESSONS AND LEGACIES: THE UNFINISHED WAR
                AND ITS AFTERMATH
                Emerson: <u>Winners and Losers</u> (excerpts)
                Young, ch. 15 / Documents 64

                FINAL EXAMINATION

Assignments: Choose A <u>or</u> B for TWO of the following options:

I A.   Write a 7-10 page paper based on a memoir, an oral
        history collection, a novel, or a collection of poems
        that focuses on an individual's or a group's
        experiences during and after the war.

I B.   Interview someone involved with the war and write up
        his or her narrative along with an analysis and
        interpretation of it.

II A.   Develop an extended essay describing your own Vietnam
        experience along with an analysis of its significance.

II B.   Write a research paper that explores a legal, moral, or
        ethical issue related to the war.

III A. Write a paper on your experience of visiting the Vietnam
        Veterans Memorial. Discuss your thoughts and feelings
        about the experience.

III B. Keep a reading journal, noting your responses to books
        and films you encounter throughout the course.

Grades: Midterm = 30%; Final = 30%; Papers (collectively) = 30%;
        Classwork = 10%

Chapter **4**

Getting to Know Your Instructors

Chapter Highlights

This chapter deals with academic interactions between students and faculty inside and outside the classroom. It addresses concerns of classroom etiquette, and it offers advice about conferring with instructors. The chapter also includes some suggestions for avoiding situations that could result in sexual harassment. Additional topics include the following:

- Discussion of academic ranks and departments
- Guidance on choosing instructors and advisors
- Information about seeking academic assistance
- Advice on asking questions in class and in conference

Key Questions

Spend a few minutes considering the following key questions.

1. What do you consider the ideal relationship between instructors and students?
2. How do you interact with your instructors? And how do they interact with you?
3. Do you have an advisor? How might you benefit from changing your advisor or having an additional advisor?

4. What qualities does your ideal instructor possess? Why do you prefer these qualities in an instructor?
5. What qualities in instructors do you dislike? Why?

The most important academic relationships you will establish in college are those with your instructors. College instructors typically design their own courses, deciding on what to include in the course and how to approach the course material. They teach you and test you on what they teach. They set the requirements and the standards for the satisfactory fulfillment of those requirements. In addition, they (or one of their assistants) will talk with you individually about your work in the course. And, finally, your instructors will grade your performance.

It pays to know your instructors. Begin by learning how to pronounce and spell each of your instructor's names. No instructor likes to receive an assignment with his or her name misspelled. (You'd be surprised how often this happens.) And learn your instructor's preferred mode of address. Some teachers insist on being addressed as "Doctor"; others prefer "Professor." Some use Mr. or Mrs. or Ms. If you are unsure how to address one of your instructors, it is safest to use "Professor." Avoid using Mr. or Ms., and avoid using first names, unless the instructor encourages such use. If you find it hard to call a fiftyish teacher Sue or Joe, stick with Professor Gannon.

Knowing the Academic Ranks

College teachers take their places in an academic hierarchy. Aside from part-time instructors, many of whom are adjunct, or auxilliary, faculty, full-time faculty members generally hold one of the following ranks, given in descending order of status:

Professor (sometimes called Full professor)
Associate professor

Taking Stock

Can you spell correctly the names of all your instructors? Do you know their first names or have any interest in knowing them? Do you know how each of your instructors prefers being addressed? How do you wish your instructors to address you?

Assistant professor
Lecturer
Instructor (in some institutions instructors outrank lecturers)
Teaching assistant (sometimes called graduate assistant)

These academic ranks have absolutely no bearing on the quality of teaching. Excellent, good, average, and bad teachers exist at every rank. What earns faculty promotions from one rank to another at research institutions is professional activity, usually in the form of research and publication. In fact, depending on the faculty teaching load at your school and on the requirements for promotion and tenure (academic security in the form of continued employment), it is likely that some, and possibly many, of your instructors will spend as much time on research, publishing, consulting, and other forms of professional activity as they do on teaching and conferring with students. This is not all bad, even from the standpoint of students, since the research that faculty publish and the conferences they attend influence their courses and enter into their conversations with students.

From time to time you will find that a faculty member's research and professional obligations necessitate rescheduling a conference or missing a class. Overall, you should be wary of faculty whose devotion to research or consulting is so intense that they invest little effort in teaching and less in helping their students learn. Most faculty care about the subjects they teach. They became college teachers because they enjoy sharing their knowledge with others, students as well as colleagues. Faculty members typically enjoy their work.

The important thing to realize is that faculty have additional responsibilities beyond preparing and teaching their classes. In addition to keeping up with research in their fields, many also have various administrative and committee responsibilities within their departments and in the university overall.

Exercise 4-1

Interview two of your instructors to ascertain their academic rank, their teaching load, and other academic or administrative responsibilities. What are their professional priorities? Or substitute an interview with an administrator such as a dean or vice president, an assistant dean, assistant vice-president, or assistant provost for one instructor interview. Find out if he or she holds an academic rank and what its associated responsibilities are.

Instructor 1 _____

Rank _____

Teaching load _____

Responsibilities _____

Instructor 2 _____

Rank _____

Teaching load _____

Responsibilities _____

Notes on Academic Departments

Faculty are grouped in departments organized according to academic field or discipline. These departments exist within individual schools. A school of business will usually include departments of accounting, finance, management, and marketing. In addition, a school of business may be affiliated with departments such as economics or law. A school of arts and sciences typically includes many more departments than does a business school, everything from anthropology to zoology.

Typically, each department offers one or more major concentrations and possibly one or more minors as well. From your standpoint as a student, once you declare your major, you need to learn "who's who" within your department or college (in the case of business or pharmacy, for example). You should realize that each college or university department, in whichever school it is situated, fulfills two primary academic functions. First, the department offers courses and services to students who are satisfying basic university requirements. Second, it services students who choose that department for the major. In addition, you can also expect advice about your business and academic future from faculty in your major. Faculty are often generous with their advice about future prospects within the university and the professions. And some faculty have very good contacts that may help you land a job or an internship.

Within departments, particularly large departments, you will find smaller divisions. An English department, for example, may include programs in writing or in American culture. Within a large History department, you might find a program in Soviet or Latin American studies. Often, however, instead of small programs or institutes situated within departments, you will find interdepartmental programs such as American Studies, International Studies, Women's Studies, African-American Studies, and Gay or Lesbian Studies. Depending on the university, these interdisciplinary programs may be departments in their own right or they may be set up as programs drawing faculty from other existing departments.

On occasion, you will find two or more departments teaming up to offer a course. Such interdepartmental cooperative efforts can be exciting for both students and participating faculty. There is no single model for team-taught interdisciplinary courses. They can be taught at the basic or required core level, but they can be also offered as advanced electives for majors. Depending on your interests and academic inclinations, you may wish to explore your university's interdepartmental or interdisciplinary course offerings. You may also wish to look into special programs such as Women's Studies.

Choosing Your Instructors

Sometimes you have little if any choice of instructor. Your schedule may require you to take Sociology 101 on Monday and Wednesday mornings, when only one section is offered. Or you may find only a single section offered of a course required for your major. With multisection courses, you may register at a time when only a single section is open. In these and similar cases you may simply have to register for what's available. There will be occasions, however, when you can choose one course or instructor over another to satisfy a major or course requirement.

How do you choose, when you have such options available? You can go by the instructor's official reputation. You can be guided by student course evaluations. You can go by hearsay. You can also meet the instructor yourself, request a syllabus, and act on your impressions and instincts.

Some professors have well-deserved reputations as prominent scholars in their fields. Although this distinction does not necessarily make those professors good teachers, you may want to take a course with one such authority for the experience alone. But you would be wise to use additional information before choosing. Besides a reputation for scholarship, consider what kinds of student evaluations a professor has received. How is he or she spoken about around the department? By the administrative assistants? By student aides who work for the department? By more advanced students majoring in the discipline? By graduate students? By other undergraduates? The more you can find out, the better your chances of making a compatible choice. Be aware, however, that what you are looking for in a professor may be different from what your friends look for.

Don't rule out setting up an appointment to speak with a professor. You can ask about an upcoming course, and you can explain your interest in the subject. And while you converse, form your own estimate not only of the specific course requirements, but also of the instructor. Attend to the instructor's manner. Does he or she listen well? Treat you nicely? Give you sufficient time? Seem preoccupied? Rush you? Patronize you? Encourage you? Exhibit interest in you and your concerns? Seem distant, remote, detached? Read the professor and make your own decision.

Exercise 4-2

Get a jump on planning for next term's courses. Talk to an instructor whose course you would like to take and ask about his or her teaching schedule. Or visit the chair or scheduling person of a department you wish to take a course in. See what you can find out about the schedule for next term's course offerings. Ask to see some course outlines.

Asking Questions in Class and Out

Some instructors encourage students to ask questions in class; others discourage it. Some instructors lecture for the full class period; others generate discussion throughout. You'll have to take your cue from the instructor's teaching style as well as from the size of the class and the kinds of response student questions receive. If you have questions, ask them.

Under the best of circumstances, an instructor will allow time for student questions even in a large lecture course. You should not be afraid to ask about something you need clarified. Nor should you be afraid to introduce an additional line of inquiry or a related point from your reading. Your questions can give an instructor a clearer sense of how well he or she is communicating essential concepts and issues. Your questions can also remind an instructor of something intended for inclusion but omitted by accident. And your questions can also stimulate others to ask their questions, from which the instructor's and students' additional response and discussion can enrich the understanding of all.

If you can't get your questions answered in class, raise them after class, preferably right away if a brief answer will suffice. If not, then consider asking

---

Taking Stock

Look back at your classroom experience for the past week. In how many classes did you ask questions? How often were your questions answered to your satisfaction?

the instructor for an appointment to discuss some of your questions, preferably before the next class. (Or go to his or her office during regularly scheduled—and posted—office hours.) It's much better to get your questions answered than to leave them hanging. Your anxiety level will decrease; you will understand things better; and the instructor may even perceive you as an eager and industrious student.

Exercise 4-3

Make a point of asking a question or two in each of your upcoming classes. For at least one class, stay after briefly to ask your instructor a question. In another class, ask for an appointment to discuss a few additional questions.

Seeking Help

If you are having trouble in a course, whether that trouble be related to understanding difficult concepts, to completing projects or papers on schedule, or adjusting to the social or intellectual climate in the classroom, speak to the instructor about it. Even in a small class, an instructor can't read students' minds. If you need help, don't be afraid to request it. Chances are if you are experiencing difficulty, other students are as well.

Don't be afraid to ask for an appointment. Let the instructor know what you do understand and identify precisely where your trouble lies. Ask the instructor for advice about what else you can do beyond attending to his or her explanations. Perhaps other readings will help you. Perhaps you can use the university's academic skills center, where student or faculty tutoring may be available.

Conferring with Instructors

Whether your instructor requires conferences as a regular part of the course requirements or whether you seek an appointment, you should be aware of some ground rules for student-teacher conferences.

First, remember that you are visiting an instructor in his or her departmental office, as this will be the most likely meeting place. There may be one or more other instructors at their desks sharing the office. At times there may be one or more additional students in the room having their own conferences with their instructors. If so, try to avoid listening in on their conferences as you would hope they would respect your privacy as well. Concentrate on your own concerns and your teacher's comments.

Second, be clear about how long the meeting will last. Many appointments with students are scheduled with the understanding that it will last anywhere from 5 minutes to an hour or more. Most student-teacher conferences fall somewhere between these extremes. It's useful to have a sense of how much time your meeting will last. A clear understanding about time limit can alleviate feelings of being shortchanged. Third, make effective and efficient use of your time with the instructor. Rather than chit-chatting about extraneous matters (unless, of course, there is no time limit), get down to business. Are you there to discuss a topic for a draft of a paper? Are you meeting to review a midterm test? To plan a long-range project? Then come prepared to work. Be ready with your paper and your questions about it. Be able to offer some suggested topics for consideration. Have that test with you and be ready with some specific questions about your answers and the instructor's grading of them. Give the instructor some evidence that you've thought about the long-range project, perhaps bringing a set of notes or questions about it. Prepare for the conference as you would prepare for an interview or a class.

Fourth, observe rules of academic etiquette. Don't assume, for example, that you can eat or smoke during a conference. And don't assume that because you and the teacher are meeting one to one that the conversation will necessarily be more informal than the professor's usual classroom style and manner. (It may be, but not necessarily.) Generally, it's wise to behave and speak as you would in class. If the conversation is to be more relaxed, it will be easy enough to downshift into informality. Take your cue from the instructor.

Fifth, if you feel the need for greater privacy, you can ask for it. But be aware that the instructor may wish to leave the door open or may even refuse to be in a room alone with a student. This practice will have less to do with you personally than with changing attitudes toward student-teacher relationships, especially in the wake of various sexual harassment charges that students have brought against faculty, sometimes justifiably and sometimes not.

Taking Stock

Think back over your last conference with one of your instructors. How did it go? How would you characterize its tone and manner? Were you satisfied with the conference? Why or why not? What do you think would have improved the conference from your standpoint?

Exercise 4-4

Schedule a conference about a specific topic with an instructor, if you can. Or simply attend your next regularly scheduled appointment with one of your instructors. During the conference, observe the guidelines described earlier. Take your cue from the instructor about the pace, duration, and level of formality of the conference.

The Problem of Sexual Harassment

Teachers are authority figures with power over students; some of them may occasionally use their authority unfairly. Since such abuses are rare, you should not expect your teachers to overpower you with their authority. On the other hand, you can expect that if a point of disagreement occurs, an instructor may rely on academic expertise or experience to close off a discussion. But you should also be alert to the possibility that a real abuse of authority can occur.

One of the more harmful aspects of such abuses of power is the trading of grades for sexual favors. Though this, too, is rare, it does occur. Sometimes this kind of bartering is initiated by the teacher, sometimes by the student. In either case it is dangerous and destructive to academic integrity and to any chance of developing a genuinely productive student-teacher relationship.

A serious problem with any kind of abuse of the student-teacher relationship, from whichever side, is the prospect that signals given by one will be misconstrued and misunderstood by the other. Looks, gestures, smiles, touches can all be intended to mean one thing yet be taken to mean something else. Our society is currently wrestling with the definition of acceptable forms of behavior between men and women in professional situations. In universities, one form of this concern involves what may be considered an acceptable range of intimacy between student and teacher. It is wisest for teachers and students to err on the side of formality rather than on a possibly dangerous friendliness that might be misconstrued as excessive intimacy. It's better to observe propriety than flirt with possible trouble. This does not mean, however, that you must be standoffish and cold in your relations with your instructors—or they with you. But be alert for possible dangers. By all means, familiarize yourself with your school's policy on sexual harassment.

Technically, *sexual harassment* is defined as unwelcome, unwanted, persistent, threatening behavior of a sexual nature of one party toward another. The issue of harassment frequently turns on whether the harasser holds a position of power or authority over the person harassed. In such instances, one person is at the mercy of another more powerful individual, who may be a boss or supervisor, or who may simply be someone with enough power to exert

---

Taking Stock

Have you ever felt uncomfortable in the presence of an instructor? If so, what made you uncomfortable? What did you do or say? Would you act or speak differently in similar circumstances today? Why or why not? Whom would you speak to if you felt sexually harassed by an instructor? What is your school's policy on sexual harassment?

---

pressure favorably or unfavorably on the weaker person's behalf. This power relationship exists between students and faculty. As authority figures in the university and as teachers, the latter have a degree of control over students by means of grades and recommendations that can be used as weapons or bargaining chips in gaining sexual favors.

Problems of sexual harassment can occur throughout a university community—between students, between faculty, and between students and staff as well as between faculty and students. One of the more persistent problems in colleges is that men and women do not always understand each other in matters of sexual contact. More than one recent instance of unwarranted sexual advance or attention has resulted in a charge of sexual harassment. And even more seriously, charges of rape have been leveled against some college men in situations where misunderstanding, alcohol, and sexual flirtation combined resulted in sexual intercourse that was not seen as mutually consensual by both parties.

Exercise 4-5

The following short story by Ernest Hemingway describes a situation of sexual intimacy. Read the story carefully, and then decide what you think each of the parties wanted from their encounter and to what extent each appears satisfied with the outcome. Discuss with your roommates, teacher, and/or classmates the extent to which sexual harassment is an issue in the story.

Up in Michigan

Jim Gilmore came to Hortons Bay from Canada. He bought the blacksmith shop from old man Horton. Jim was short and dark with big mustaches and big hands. He was a good horseshoer and did not look much like a blacksmith even with his leather apron on. He lived upstairs above the blacksmith shop and took his meals at D. J. Smith's.

Liz Coates worked for Smith's. Mrs. Smith, who was a very large clean woman, said Liz Coates was the neatest girl she'd ever seen. Liz had good legs and always wore clean gingham aprons and Jim noticed that her hair was always neat behind. He liked her face because it was so jolly but he never thought about her.

Liz liked Jim very much. She liked it the way he walked over from the shop and often went to the kitchen door to watch for him to start down the road. She liked it about his mustache. She liked it about how white his teeth were when he smiled. She liked it very much that he didn't look like a blacksmith. She liked it how much D. J. Smith and Mrs. Smith liked Jim. One day she found that she liked it the way the hair was black on his arms and how white they were above the tanned line when he washed up in the washbasin outside the house. Liking that made her feel funny.

Hortons Bay, the town, was only five houses on the main road between Boyne City and Charlevoix. There was the general store and post office with a high false front and maybe a wagon hitched out in front, Smith's house, Stroud's house, Dilworth's house, Horton's house and Van Hoosen's house. The houses were in a big grove of elm trees and the road was very sandy. There was farming country and timber each way up the road. Up the road a ways was the Methodist church and down the road the other direction was the township school. The blacksmith shop was painted red and faced the school.

A steep sandy road ran down the hill to the bay through the timber. From Smith's back door you could look out across the woods that ran down to the lake and across the bay. It was very beautiful in the spring and summer, the bay blue and bright and usually whitecaps on the lake out beyond the point from the breeze blowing from Charlevoix and Lake Michigan. From Smith's back door Liz could see ore barges way out in the lake going toward Boyne City. When she looked at them they didn't seem to be moving at all but if she went in and dried some more dishes and then came out again they would be out of sight beyond the point.

All the time now Liz was thinking about Jim Gilmore. He didn't seem to notice her much. He talked about the shop to D. J. Smith and about the Republican Party and about James G. Blaine. In the evenings he read *The Toledo Blade* and the Grand Rapids paper by the lamp in the front room or went out spearing fish in the bay with a jacklight with D. J. Smith. In the fall he and Smith and Charley Wyman took a wagon and tent, grub, axes, their rifles and two dogs and went on a trip to the pine plains beyond Vanderbilt deer hunting. Liz and Mrs. Smith were cooking for four days for them before they started. Liz wanted to make something special for Jim to take but she didn't finally because she was afraid to ask Mrs. Smith for the eggs and flour and afraid if she bought them Mrs. Smith would catch her cooking. It would have been all right with Mrs. Smith but Liz was afraid.

All the time Jim was gone on the deer hunting trip Liz thought about him. It was awful while he was gone. She couldn't sleep well from thinking about him but she discovered it was fun to think about him too. If she let herself go it was better. The night before they were to come back she didn't sleep at all, that is she didn't think she slept because it was all mixed up in a dream about not sleeping and really not sleeping. When she saw the wagon coming down the road she felt weak and sick sort of inside. She couldn't wait till she saw Jim and it seemed as though everything would be all right when he came. The wagon stopped outside under the big elm and Mrs. Smith and Liz went out. All the men had beards and there were three deer in the back of the wagon, their thin legs sticking stiff over the edge of the wagon box. Mrs. Smith kissed D. J. and he hugged her. Jim said "Hello, Liz," and grinned. Liz hadn't known just what would happen when Jim got back but she was sure it would be something. Nothing had happened. The men were just home, that was all. Jim pulled the burlap sacks off the deer and Liz looked at them. One was a big buck. It was stiff and hard to lift out of the wagon.

"Did you shoot it, Jim?" Liz asked.

"Yeah. Ain't it a beauty ?" Jim got it onto his back to carry to the smokehouse.

That night Charley Wyman stayed to supper at Smith's. It was too late to get back to Charlevoix. The men washed up and waited in the front room for supper.

"Ain't there something left in that crock, Jimmy?" D. J. Smith asked, and Jim went out to the wagon in the barn and fetched in the jug of whiskey the men had taken hunting with them. It was a four-gallon jug and there was quite a little slopped back and forth in the bottom. Jim took a long pull on his way back to the house. It was hard to lift such a big jug up to drink out of it. Some of the whiskey ran down on his shirt front. The two men smiled when Jim came in with the jug. D. J. Smith sent for glasses and Liz brought them. D. J. poured out three big shots.

"Well, here's looking at you, D. J.," said Charley Wyman.

"That damn big buck, Jimmy," said D. J.

"Here's all the ones we missed, D. J.," said Jim, and downed his liquor.

"Tastes good to a man."

"Nothing like it this time of year for what ails you."

"How about another, boys?"

"Here's how, D. J."

"Down the creek, boys."

"Here's to next year."

Jim began to feel great. He loved the taste and the feel of whiskey. He was glad to be back to a comfortable bed and warm food and the shop. He had another drink. The men came in to supper feeling hilarious but acting very respectable. Liz sat at the table after she put on the food and ate with the family. It was a good dinner. The men ate seriously. After supper they went into the front room again and Liz cleaned off with Mrs. Smith. Then Mrs. Smith went upstairs and pretty soon Smith came out and went upstairs too. Jim and Charley were still in the front room. Liz was sitting in the kitchen next to the stove pretending to read a book and thinking about Jim. She didn't want to go to bed yet because she knew Jim would be coming out and she wanted to see him as he went out so she could take the way he looked up to bed with her.

She was thinking about him hard and then Jim came out. His eyes were shining and his hair was a little rumpled. Liz looked down at her book. Jim came over back of her chair and stood there and she could feel him breathing and then he put his arms around her. Her breasts felt plump and firm and the nipples were erect under his hands. Liz was terribly frightened, no one had ever touched her, but she thought, "He's come to me finally. He's really come."

She held herself stiff because she was so frightened and did not know anything else to do and then Jim held her tight against the chair and kissed her. It was such a sharp, aching, hurting feeling that she thought she couldn't stand it. She felt Jim right through the back of the chair and she couldn't stand it and then something clicked inside of her and the feeling was warmer and softer. Jim held her tight hard against the chair and she wanted it now and Jim whispered, "Come on for a walk."

Liz took her coat off the peg on the kitchen wall and they went out the door. Jim had his arm around her and every little way they stopped and pressed against each other and Jim kissed her. There was no moon and they walked ankle-deep in the sandy road through the trees down to the dock and the warehouse on the bay. The water was lapping in the piles and the point was dark across the bay. It was cold but Liz was hot all over from being with Jim. They sat down in the shelter of the warehouse and Jim pulled Liz close to him. She was frightened. One of Jim's hands went inside her dress and stroked over her breast and the other hand was in her lap. She was very frightened and didn't know how he was going to go about things but she snuggled close to him. Then the hand that felt so big in her lap went away and was on her leg and started to move up it.

"Don't, Jim," Liz said. Jim slid the hand further up.

"You mustn't, Jim. You mustn't." Neither Jim nor Jim's big hand paid any attention to her.

The boards were hard. Jim had her dress up and was trying to do something to her. She was frightened but she wanted it. She had to have it but it frightened her.

"You mustn't do it, Jim. You mustn't."

"I got to. I'm going to. You know we got to."

"No we haven't, Jim. We ain't got to. Oh, it isn't right. Oh, it's so big and it hurts so. You can't. Oh, Jim. Jim. Oh."

The hemlock planks of the dock were hard and splintery and cold and Jim was heavy on her and he had hurt her. Liz pushed him, she was so uncomfortable and cramped. Jim was asleep. He wouldn't move. She worked out from under him and sat up and straightened her skirt and coat and tried to do something with her hair. Jim was sleeping with his mouth a little open. Liz leaned over and kissed him on the cheek. He was still asleep. She lifted his head a little and shook it. He rolled his head over and swallowed. Liz started to cry. She walked over to the edge of the dock and looked down to the water. There was a mist coming up from the bay. She was cold and miserable and everything felt gone. She walked back to where Jim was lying and shook him once more to make sure. She was crying.

"Jim," she said, "Jim. Please, Jim."

Jim stirred and curled a little tighter. Liz took off her coat and leaned over and covered him with it. She tucked it around him neatly and carefully. Then she walked across the dock and up the steep sandy road to go to bed. A cold mist was coming up through the woods from the bay.

Dealing with Instructors You Don't Like

It is unlikely that you will like all your college instructors. As with your contacts in life generally, your relationships with instructors will vary. Some you will like and feel comfortable with; others you probably won't. You shouldn't worry if you don't like every instructor. More important than your subjective response to your teachers is that you learn what they have to teach.

If you have difficulty approaching an instructor because you feel either disliked or intimidated, consider asking another teacher you are more comfortable with about how you might improve the relationship. Avoid complaining about a teacher you don't especially like to others whose classes you do enjoy. Instead, explain that you have a problem relating to Professor X or understanding Professor Y and seek advice about how to improve matters.

Consider too, visiting your problem professor during office hours, perhaps inviting a classmate whose situation is similar to yours to come along. The support of a third party might bolster your confidence. Most important of all, try to open the channels of communication. Let the professor see that you are a concerned and committed student who takes the course seriously and who wants to learn.

If you can't make progress, however, and feel you are being mistreated by an instructor, don't simply take it. Try discussing the matter openly with the instructor. If this doesn't help, consult the appropriate departmental administrator. Many situations, such as grade disputes or unfair treatment of particular students, are resolved at the departmental level. For more complicated issues, visit the office of the academic dean. The chairperson of the appropriate department should be able to advise you how to proceed beyond the department. In cases where the chairperson makes problems worse, you can simply contact the dean's office and find out how to proceed with your complaint.

The Absent Professor

Not every professor or instructor keeps regular office hours. Some scarcely ever hold them, preferring to schedule meetings by appointment only. This may violate university or departmental policy. If an instructor holds no regular office hours and avoids scheduling office appointments, you will have to make a greater effort to secure a meeting. Once you do, you should keep it, and you should expect the instructor to extend you the same courtesy.

If your instructor fails to keep appointments, and if you cannot secure a satisfactory explanation, you may have to take the problem to the department chair or to a dean. If the university requires instructors to meet with students, then faculty should not be permitted to avoid that responsibility. If office hours are supposed to be posted or otherwise publicized, then it is within your rights to ask the instructor or department for a list of those times. If the hours are not routinely kept, and if you cannot achieve satisfaction in your efforts to communicate with the instructor, it may be time for a complaint to the appropriate academic authority.

Most instructors, happily, post their office hours and keep them. In the event that they can't keep a normally posted office time, they will inform a secretary or post a note. If they forget from time to time, they will be careful to ensure that students are provided with another scheduled meeting.

When you are unsuccessful in scheduling an office visit, or when you need help that perhaps another instructor can provide, take your problem to a sympathetic teacher or administrator and seek his or her help. That individual may be able to provide you with the assistance you need. Such individuals will usually find a way to direct you to someone who can help you if they can't do it themselves. You also have the additional option of explaining your problem to the department chair and asking for another faculty member to assist you.

Professors As Advisors

As with teachers, so with advisors: some are excellent, others not so good. More than one student has received mistaken information from an advisor and bad advice based on it. You will need to decide on your advisors in the same way you decide upon teachers and courses. Don't be afraid to ask who the best advisors are. Check with other students. Talk to the secretaries and administrative assistants. Ask the department chair. As you do with your teachers, trust your instincts. Perhaps you can even ask a teacher to be your "unofficial" advisor.

Most instructors are happy to help students. In the capacity of official advisor, an instructor may be assigned to assist a specific number of majors. Usually the department makes such assignments, but you can request a particular faculty member as an advisor as well. On occasions and under circumstances where such a request cannot be accommodated, you can work with the advisor you are assigned and then informally ask for additional advice from faculty members you know better or are more comfortable with. If you do this, be sure to let them know who your official advisor is and what advice this faculty member has given you.

Even though your advisor's official role will be to assist you with fulfilling your academic requirements, you may receive other kinds of help as well.

Although most teachers consider it unprofessional to criticize the quality of their colleagues' research and teaching, they may encourage you to meet with particular faculty members for informal discussion or to enroll in their courses. If you trust your advisor, you should seriously consider doing what he or she suggests.

Your advisor can help you decide about academic alternatives you may need to consider: whether to change majors, whether to transfer to another school, whether to take summer courses, to travel or work. In short, don't be afraid to consult your advisor about other issues.

Think of your advisor as another teacher. Whether or not you actually take a course with this faculty member, you can learn from your advisor about his or her specialty. Your advisor is an important academic resource. Don't hesitate to seek advice on paper topics, outside readings, plans for graduate or professional study, or any other academic concern.

In addition, once you get to know your advisor you'll discover that besides a particular academic specialty, he or she will possess other interests and areas of unofficial expertise. He or she may be an avid music lover or a former athlete. Your advisor may be fluent in one or more languages, have traveled extensively, be an outstanding cook, piano player, skier, computer whiz. And like most people who know a lot about something outside their profession, your advisor will probably be more than happy to talk with you about his or her enthusiasms. You should not be reluctant to enjoy the benefits of your advisor's knowledge and experience with additional interests outside the professional setting of college.

To benefit from the help of an advisor, try to work together over an extended period. Try to avoid changing advisors too often, since frequent changes can disrupt your ability to do long-term planning. And remember that even though an advisor can help you with academic questions and problems, ultimately you are responsible for your own education. It is your responsibility to pay attention to your college's graduation requirements and to the requirements you must meet to complete your major. And don't forget about extracurricular activities that will enrich and enhance your degree.

Exercise 4-6

Consider how you might get to know your advisor better. Drop by for a brief informal office-hour visit. Schedule an appointment to discuss a more substantive academic issue.

Chapter 5

Learning about College Support Services

Chapter Highlights

All colleges and universities have support services to help students with a wide range of needs, from health care and psychological counseling to assistance with math and writing through tutoring and skills centers. This chapter focuses on academic support services and on related cocurricular resources available at most schools. Topics and areas covered include

- Writing and academic skills centers
- Computer and language labs
- Career planning and counseling services
- Internships
- Workshops and tutorials
- Clubs and other cocurricular activities

Key Questions

1. Do you know where to find your school's writing or academic skills center? What are its days and hours of operation? Who staffs it, and what do you have to do to use its services?
2. Where are the computer and language labs? What are their hours of operation? When are they most heavily used?

3. What counseling services does your school offer? Where are those services located? How do you use them?

4. Where can you find information on workshops on such topics as stress and time management, study skills, and writing research papers?

5. Which clubs and other cocurricular activities interest you?

Taking Advantage of Your School's Services

Some students go through college rarely using the many academic resources available to them. Don't let this happen to you. Since part of your tuition pays for skills centers, language and computer labs, counseling and tutorial services, and perhaps other resources, you should take advantage of them.

Although you are most likely aware that education occurs beyond classroom and library walls, you may not always see the connections that exist between cocurricular activities and your more strictly academic work. Cocurricular activities provide excellent opportunities for you to further your education, academic and otherwise. Some cocurricular activities such as a math club or school radio station may be included as part of a course requirement or they may simply enhance your understanding of material you are learning in related courses. Other cocurricular opportunities such as a chess club, volunteer organization, or an orchestra may provide occasions to meet like-minded individuals with whom you can develop lasting friendships.

The first thing to do, of course, is learn just what kinds of support services and cocurricular activities are available at your school. Find out *where* student support services are located, who supervises them, and when you can use them. Find out where student clubs and organizations meet or have their offices. Some services permit drop-in visits; others require scheduled appointments. Often offices and programs publicize their special services around campus on bulletin boards, on kiosks, and in student newspapers. All will have office and phone listings in the university directory. Call for information, stop in for a brief visit, and read and hang onto the flyers and brochures that list their various services and hours. If you don't plan to use the information early in the year, set it aside in a file or on a shelf for easy access when you need it.

Along with services such as the computer lab or writing center, be alert also for workshops, tutoring sessions, minicourses, and other special services your school offers. You may wish to attend workshops on writing research papers, studying efficiently, or handling academic pressures. You may want to attend a talk or discussion on drugs, drinking, date rape, race relations on campus, or some other concern.

Taking Stock

What academic support services does your university provide? Is there a tutoring center? A writing or math skills center? A computer lab? A language lab? Where are these support services located? Who runs them?

What other kinds of support services—not strictly academic ones—does your school provide? Where can you go for psychological or spiritual counseling? Where is the infirmary or health center?

What are the phone numbers and hours you can contact someone for help?

Seek out the job placement and career services office. You may wish to secure a cooperative education position or an internship that involves part-time work during the academic year with prospects for full-time summer employment or an entry-level position after you graduate. Talk to faculty members, especially those with connections in the outside world.

These basic services will be available in varying degrees depending on the kind of school you attend, the size of its student body, and the amount of funding it secures. Whether the services come from one office or many, and whether they are heavily or lightly funded, you can generally expect to find a range of special services that offer guidance on matters physical, psychological, spiritual, social, and academic. Since your academic performance will be affected by your general well-being, don't think of these support services as unrelated to your academic work. Consider them instead as aids to academic success.

These and other university resources are sources of academic capital available for your expenditure and use. Sometimes students avoid capitalizing on their school's richest resources partly out of ignorance and partly from an insufficient sense of their purposes, functions, and potential value. Many students consider the writing lab, for example, as only a place for poor writers, or the job placement center as only for seniors. This is a mistake. These services offer more than you might imagine. Look into them all.

Exercise 5-1

Identify the location and hours of the following academic resources.

Writing center _____

Math lab _____

Computer facilities _____

Tutoring services _____

Language lab _____

Libraries _____

Religious counseling _____

Psychological counseling _____

Student service office _____

Food services _____

Bookstore _____

Copy center _____

Coop education _____

Infirmary/Health center _____

Study abroad _____

Others _____

Writing Centers

Your writing center may be staffed by full-time faculty or staff and also by part-time faculty and student peer tutors. You can benefit from the working relationship you establish with those who work in them.

One of the most pervasive misconceptions students have about writing centers is to see them merely as places for remediation. Although to assist students who need extra help may be one of a writing center's functions, it is certainly not the only one. Nor is it likely to be the most important. Consider the writing center instead as a place where writing is taken seriously, a place to obtain reactions to what you've written, suggestions for what you are working on but have not yet written, and ideas for revision, at whatever stage your paper or project may be. Look to the center as a place you can go for additional response to your work from trained people who care about writing. You will find students and teachers on the center's staff who are eager and able to read your drafts and suggest ways to improve them. You will find books and articles, flyers and brochures containing useful ideas and helpful tips. See the writing center as an opportunity for academic growth, not as an emergency unit to visit only when you receive a negative grade on one of your papers.

Your writing center may provide services you never thought about. At some schools, for example, staff members hold evening tutorials in students' living quarters. Writing center staff leave their central quarters and go out to where the students are, making themselves available for consultation and advice on papers and reports. But that's only one example. Your school's writing center may provide this and other services. It might be a good idea for you to make use of such services even as early as your first required writing assignments become due.

Exercise 5-2

Visit your school's writing center and find out what services are provided and how you can use them. Make an appointment to discuss some writing you have done or will be doing later in the term. Have specific goals in mind when you go (to plan the organization of a paper, for example, or to work toward correcting errors of grammar or punctuation in a paper or report).

Other Academic Skills Centers

Besides a writing center, your college may provide other skills centers. These may all be coordinated under a single staff member. They may also be part of a single comprehensive university resource center with a name like "Academic Support Services" or "Academic Skills Center." Or perhaps your college keeps its skills and study centers separate, affiliating them with academic departments. You can find out easily enough. It shouldn't matter, however, since your concern is simply to discover what services the various centers provide and how you might use them effectively.

More than likely, you will find support services for reading and mathematics as well as for writing. Sometimes reading and math support services may be directly connected to courses in the curriculum. Often such courses are designed to help students gain the competence and confidence they need to perform successfully in more advanced courses. If you think you might benefit from some intensive groundwork, you should arrange a meeting and set up a course of study at the appropriate center. If you have been assigned to one of the centers based on test scores, or if you use its services in conjunction with a developmental course in math or reading, try to make the most of the opportunity. These centers and these courses have been designed to increase your chances to succeed in college. They can provide you with the skills as well as the confidence you'll need for successful academic performance.

You may even wish to think of such academic support services as another "class" to enhance your learning.

Exercise 5-3

Find out what specific academic support services your school has and where you can get extra help in one of the following subjects: writing, math, accounting, economics, physics, engineering, nursing, computer science. Sign up for extra help in one of these subjects with a peer or faculty tutor. Prepare for your visit by jotting down questions and going over problems for which you would find additional explanation helpful.

Computer and Language Labs

Unless you have your own computer, you will find the university computer lab an extremely important resource. There you will find computers available for student use. You will probably also find many students vying for computer time. If you know that you will be using the computer center to draft and revise your written assignments, find out from the staff not only when the center is open, but also when it is used most heavily (and perhaps more important, when it is used most lightly). Find out whether you can simply drop in and set to work, or whether you must schedule an appointment for a specific time slot.

If you have your own computer, find out how to link up with the university computer. Visit the computer lab for specific information on using its facilities and services.

Another thing you'll need to look into is the availability of printers and whether there is any charge for printing out your work. Find out, too, whether the computer center offers instruction in the use of its equipment and programs, the times when this instruction is offered, and how you can arrange to receive it. You may discover that the lab offers regularly scheduled tutorials or practice sessions for beginners and more advanced users of word processing programs, spreadsheets, and math programs. You may discover further that you can receive individualized instruction, perhaps at additional cost.

Exercise 5-4

Visit your school's computer center or lab. Become comfortable with its equipment, and arrange to use it to write and print out a paper. If your computer center's equipment is foreign to you, sign up for an instructional session. Also find out what software is available for use. If you need instruction in using any software, sign up for instruction.

Language Laboratories

Like the computer lab, your college language lab may become an important resource for you. And this may be the case whether or not you take language courses. Most students think of the language lab as a place only for students actually enrolled in courses. And though it's true that many students use the language lab in conjunction with their courses, other students may be able to use it as well. As with the computer lab, you'll need to know what restrictions may be put upon your use of the language lab. You should also inquire about hours of heavy and light use, and what the sign-up and sign-in procedures may be.

You can expect to find the language lab equipped with individual headphones and tape players. But you will also find books, magazines, and newspapers in the languages taught at your college, and perhaps in a few that are not. Beyond these resources you may find information about travel programs, study abroad, and additional books on the history and culture of the various peoples and nations whose languages the university includes in its curriculum.

Exercise 5-5

Visit your school's language lab. Talk to someone on staff there and ask about its resources, hours of operation, and conditions for use.

Workshops, Tutorials, Lectures

Most colleges and universities offer workshops, tutorials, meetings, and informal discussion sessions in connection with such university resources as computer and language labs; reading, writing, math, and academic skills centers; health, social, and psychological support services. Take advantage of these special meetings, classes, and information sessions. Use them as a way to increase the scope of your college experience, even if you don't feel any immediate need to enlist the services of their affiliated programs.

You will probably also hear about numerous additional cocurricular activities. Among these may be lectures given by specialists from various branches of the university faculty and by visiting luminaries from other universities as well as from the political and business worlds. There may also be occasional debates; administrative information sessions; readings of creative work produced by faculty, students, and visiting writers; and conferences, institutes, and colloquia that may last from an afternoon to a week. Such cocurricular offerings may be offered in conjunction with a particular college course or a special departmental program; they may also be run independently.

Exercise 5-6

Read the bulletin boards in your residence and dining hall as well as those in and around classroom buildings and departmental offices. Consult your school newspapers and listen to the college radio station for announcements about the array of promising cocurricular experiences. Attend a workshop, lecture, discussion, or some other cocurricular activity that interests you.

Clubs and Other Activities

What clubs exist at your college? How can you join? To what extent are the clubs officially recognized by the school? Who is in charge? Who are the members? And what benefits can be derived from participating? Answers to these and similar questions may lead you to join the staff of one of your college newspapers or literary magazines, its yearbook or radio station, its religious or service organizations, its music or theater groups, its political or social clubs.

Club membership can be an academic experience as well as a social one. It can also give you a chance to develop practical skills related to your major or your career ambitions. And it can provide you with a chance to relax and have fun doing things you enjoy. As a high school student you probably belonged to a number of clubs and pursued varied extra- and cocurricular activities. In college you will have more such opportunities on an even more ambitious scale. Consider these and other university resources in connection with your academic work and your general education. They can enrich your academic experience.

Taking Stock

List two or three clubs and organizations you might like to join. Identify how these activities fit in with your overall goals and priorities.

Career Planning

Find out what office handles career planning, job placement, internships, and the like. Find out, too, which staff members are responsible for the various services the office provides. As with the other university support services, the career planning office will require you to follow certain procedures to participate in its programs even if it is something as minor as being put on a mailing list.

Look for publicity that advertises the services of this office, whatever it is called. Make an appointment to speak with one of the counselors there. This is particularly important for an office whose services may not be as self-evident as those provided by a computer lab or a writing center. And even though you may be a first-year student, you should inquire about career planning services and internships, for you might be surprised to learn about opportunities for which you qualify even now. You might receive useful advice about how to plan for your career from experienced and knowledgeable counselors. They might start you thinking about practical aspects of your future and about possibilities you had never before considered. Such thinking could have a direct bearing on shifts among your academic interests, needs, and choices.

Using Your Imagination

Project ahead a few years and think about what career you might like to pursue. You may already be pursuing one or be clearly directed toward a specific career. In either case, make a mental list of the services you expect to find at your school's career planning office (or a similar office).

Internships

Your college or university very likely offers opportunities for you to pursue independent study. You may also be able to earn academic credit in conjunction with a part-time or full-time internship for a month, a summer, a term, or an academic year. Education majors routinely perform student teaching internships as part of their requirements toward earning state teaching certification. And nursing majors typically do clinical internships in hospitals and other care facilities toward satisfying part of their degree and state certification requirements.

Opportunities for other kinds of internships not required for degree programs or various certifications may also be available at your school. You may find, for example, that you can earn from 1 to 6 credits or more for working at a job related to your major. As an English or communications major you might be able to earn credit for working at a local newspaper, magazine, or radio station. You might serve as an editorial assistant at a publishing house or work on catalogue copy for a supplier of audio recordings of books and other materials.

Consult faculty members in your major field. Talk to administrators. Ask around among family, friends, classmates, and acquaintances. Visit the cooperative education office or other career services office at your school. And be sure to talk with older students, especially graduates, who have done such internships, to learn about their benefits and drawbacks.

Counseling and Support Services

Your college or university will offer many other kinds of support services, some of them more directly related to academic concerns than others. Since most students' physical and emotional well-being directly affects their academic performance, you might also learn about university resources that address those needs. Find out whether your college has a religious counseling center, and whether it is nondenominational or multidenominational. Perhaps religious and spiritual counseling are offered under the aegis of a psychological counseling center. Perhaps they fall under the umbrella of the university health center.

Other kinds of support, advice, and counsel may also be available, including special centers set up for women and for various racial and ethnic minorities. If such centers exist, they may be further affiliated with programs, which may be connected to the academic curriculum. Some programs exist as part of the curriculum—in Women's Studies or African-American Studies, in Classical Studies or International Studies, for example—programs that may be administratively separate from other university resources. Find out what your college offers, who is in charge, and how you can make use of their services. Perhaps you may be qualified to help provide services in one of these areas because of your background or experience.

You may find that whether or not such services are kept distinct from corollary academic programs, students and faculty involved in one will also be involved in the other. And you may discover that some of the services these additional university resources make available can make a difference not only

---

Taking Stock

Make a list of counseling and other support services your school provides. What role do you anticipate these services providing in your college career? Why?

in your overall college experience but in your academic performance and success as well.

Volunteer Organizations

Your school may also offer opportunities for you to do volunteer work. You may be able to work with children, perhaps tutoring them in English or mathematics, perhaps teaching them to swim or play basketball. There may be opportunities to do other kinds of community service, perhaps visiting the elderly in a local nursing home or helping to beautify a public park.

Some universities offer academic credit for various types of social action and volunteer work. You may be able to help build a school or work on an irrigation project in a foreign country while you learn about that country's political organization and social and economic history.

Through volunteer work you may improve your facility with a foreign language, develop your social conscience, enrich your spiritual sense of self. Besides its practical usefulness for yourself and others, volunteer work may also introduce you to others who share your values while giving you an opportunity to put into active practice some of your most cherished beliefs.

Exercise 5-7

Consult your school's promotional literature, along with print or video information about its mission and identity. See whether there is an office or program that includes opportunities for students to do volunteer work. Or talk with faculty and administrators about the prospects and availability of volunteer programs at your school.

Chapter **6**

Improving Study and Notetaking Skills

Chapter Highlights

Academic success requires good study skills outside class and good notetaking skills both in class and out. This chapter will reinforce the successful study habits and effective notetaking strategies you may already possess and introduce you to other techniques as well.

The two major sections of this chapter—on notetaking and studying—supplement and reinforce one another. Your out-of-class studying prepares you for successful in-class notetaking; your in-class notetaking enables your continued learning outside the classroom.
Topics discussed include the following:

- How to take notes efficiently
- How to organize your notes effectively
- How to concentrate and focus
- How to study successfully
- How to remember what you learn

Key Questions

1. Do you presently have a system for taking notes in class?
2. How do you take notes on material for humanities and science courses?
3. How do you organize your notes for each of your courses?

4. Do you have trouble concentrating in class? When you are studying outside class? If so, why?
5. Do you remember what you have learned? How well? For how long?

Developing Notetaking Skills

The first rule for good notetaking is to be prepared. One kind of preparation involves the studying you do before class—reading assigned chapters or pages, doing problems and exercises, bringing in drafts of written work as required. Another kind of preparation involves bringing the necessary tools to class—the right books and notebooks, pens, pencils, portable computer—whatever you need to take good notes.

Being prepared in these ways, though necessary, is not sufficient. You also need to attend to additional matters. Some, like finding a good place to sit, are simple; others, like listening attentively, are more complex and may require effort, practice, or a change in habit.

Finding a Place To Sit

Find a place in the classroom or lecture hall where you are comfortable and from which you can see and hear the instructor. The closer to the front you are, the better you will be able to see and hear and the fewer distractions you will receive from other students. Choosing a seat that is also in a well-lit area and away from a humming air conditioner or a blowing heater may require you to come a few minutes early. But being in a good spot enables you to concentrate better on classwork and makes notetaking easier. It also allows you to make frequent eye contact with the instructors, which can help them gauge your level of involvement and will help you follow their visual cues.

Listening

We often take listening for granted. But how many times have you said to someone, "You haven't heard what I was saying," or, "You aren't really

---

Taking Stock

How do you prepare yourself for each of your classes? What does each of your instructors expect? To preview a chapter or section of a textbook before class discussion? Always? Sometimes? Hardly ever? To read or study?

Taking Stock

Where do you sit in each of your courses? Do you sit in the same general area for each class? Depending on class size and the instructor's preferred way to arrange seats, do you sit near the instructor? Near friends? In a comfortable part of the room?

---

listening"? Learning how to listen is critical for academic success. You can improve your listening skills by following these guidelines.

Listening Guidelines

1. Be a willing rather than a reluctant listener.
   Expect to hear something interesting.
   Listen for the unexpected detail, the unusual example.
2. Be a focused rather than a distracted listener.
   Concentrate on what is being said. Refocus when your mind wanders.
3. Be an engaged rather than a disengaged listener.
   Find ways to connect what is said with what you know.
   Identify key points and supporting details.
   Don't stop listening out of boredom or disagreement.
4. Be an active rather than a passive listener.
   Try to anticipate where the lecture may be going at different points.
5. Ask questions about anything unclear, no matter how simple you think your question may be. Other students may have the same questions.
6. Participate as much as you can. Add your own comments to those of other students.

Exercise 6-1

For your next few classes, apply the listening guidelines just described. Then write a paragraph explaining how they affected your understanding of the class material.

Attending to Handwriting

Good class notes are legible notes. If you cannot read what you have written during a class lecture, you might just as well not have taken notes in the first place. Strive to write clearly, even if it slows you down. You may even wish to print especially important information.

If you have serious problems with handwriting, you may be able to use a notebook computer or a tape recorder. The computer, however, requires that you have good keyboarding skills. And the tape recorder may not be permitted by all your instructors. (Ask before bringing one to class.) One of the disadvantages of taping lectures is that you won't be selecting the important details for inclusion in your notes. Another disadvantage of taping is that you may not pay as close attention to what is said; moreover, you will also need to spend time later listening to the taped lecture and discussion.

The best thing, ideally, is simply to learn to write legibly. If you can, develop your own form of shorthand, even though it will require practice. This skill will help you write faster during a lecture, especially with instructors who cover a lot of ground quickly. Be careful, however, to be consistent in your use of abbreviations and symbols so that you can remember later what they stand for.

You may also wish to exchange notes with another capable student to see if you missed any key concepts or points.

Watching and Noticing

Another guideline for effective notetaking is to watch your instructor closely. Nonverbal signs, such as an instructor's facial expressions and gestures, may be used to emphasize a point. If the instructor writes something on the board or uses an overhead projector to highlight a point, be sure to write it down. Usually when instructors take the trouble to write something down—whether on the board or in a handout—they expect students to copy, study, and remember it.

Watching your instructors closely is another way to be involved and attentive in class. Your instructors expect you to pay attention to them. One way to show them that you are doing just that is by looking directly at them, making eye contact. Looking complements listening and is a way to focus and avoid distraction. You should use looking and listening as ways to identify key elements of lecture and discussion. For example, when your instructors look toward their notes, that often indicates that they are about to mention a key point or concept.

Participating in Class

Many classes require participation. The degree of participation from one course to another may vary considerably—from classes in which an occasional student asks a rare question to classes in which group discussion is the norm. Instructors differ, sometimes radically, in how they initiate or discourage class

---

Taking Stock

In which of your classes are discussion and participation required? In which are they encouraged? Are they discouraged in any? How would you assess your own level of participation? Why do you participate or avoid participating in your classes?

---

discussion. But whether or not your classes require participation, you should try to participate as fully as possible.

You can ask questions, respond to them, and comment further on discussion initiated by the instructor or by other students. By becoming actively involved in class, you keep focused, and you take better notes on the important aspects of class discussion. You also have a greater chance to remember material enlivened by class discussion, especially if you participated actively.

Notetaking Techniques

Taking notes in lecture courses involves more than trying to write down as much as you can while the instructor speaks. First, you may be physically unable to write as rapidly as your instructors speak, even if some of them speak slowly. Second, it isn't necessary to write everything down. In fact, one of the values of taking class notes is to decide what is worth recording. You need to be selective, to write down the essential concepts and ideas along with as much supporting information as enables you to understand the day's lesson.

For courses in which instructors provide well-organized lectures, simply following their lead in recording the major points made will generally result in reasonable, well-organized notes, especially if you can identify headings for your notes. In courses where instructors do not provide a clear sense of organization, you will have to work harder to take well-organized notes. The important thing is for you to sort the information and concepts in a logical way that makes sense to you.

The discussion-centered class may give you trouble in this respect. In a literature course in which you discuss a short story or novel, for example, it may not be clear just what you should record from a particular class discussion. As in a lecture class, however, you should take your cues from the instructor. Typically, the instructor leads the discussion, usually by asking questions. You should record these questions in your notes, letting the questions serve as your key aspects of the day's topic. Record any answers the instructor provides, along with those the instructor approves of and perhaps supplements or elaborates on. In discussion-centered classes in which questions do not provide a way to organize your notes, you will need to devise another way to record what seems important for learning and for taking tests. You can ask the instructor to summarize key points following a discussion. You can also record your impressions of the flow of ideas in the discussion, noting points of agreement and disagreement between the instructor and members of the class.

For both lecture and discussion classes, you may wish to use the Cornell notetaking system or the double-column notebook. Both of these notetaking strategies involve dividing your note page so that there is room for you to record your thoughts and questions as well as the information and ideas you glean from lecture and discussion. Each notetaking technique helps you to become active and thoughtful, making the material your own rather than passively absorbing it. Both notetaking techniques also encourage active engagement and critical thinking.

Using the Cornell Notetaking System

To use the Cornell notetaking system, developed by Walter Pauk of Cornell University, set up your page in the following manner:

1. Draw a line down the page 2 inches or so from the left margin.
2. Draw a second line across the page 2 inches or so from the bottom.

With your page divided into three areas, you have room to record different kinds of notes in the different areas. In the large area you record information—facts, concepts, and ideas. In the lefthand column you write questions you have about the facts and ideas you made notes on. You can also note key concepts with headlines. And in the bottom space you write a summary, condensing the essence of your notes on that page.

The value of the Cornell system is that it encourages reflection by leaving room for you to record your thoughts alongside your notes. Here is how a Cornell system note page would look with the space for each area identified.

Using a Double-Column Notebook

A second recommended notetaking technique is the double-column notebook, developed by Ann E. Berthoff, formerly of the University of Massachusetts at Boston. To create a double-column notebook page, you simply divide your

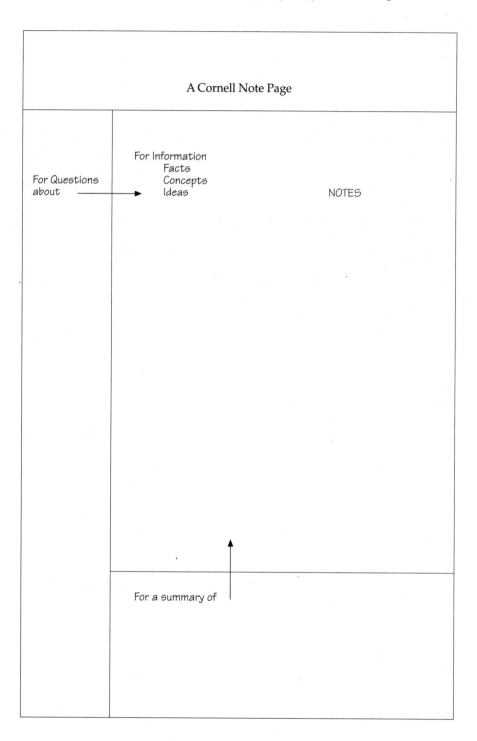

A Cornell Note Page

For Questions about

For Information
Facts
Concepts
Ideas

NOTES

For a summary of

page into two parts, roughly two-thirds for one area and one-third for the other. You can draw your dividing line either vertically or horizontally.

In the larger part of your page, you take notes, recording information and ideas. You should also summarize the speaker's (or writer's) ideas in this same space. In the smaller part of the page, you make additional notes by asking questions and making connections with other things you have heard, seen, or read. You can also write your reactions to the notes and summaries you write. The important thing is that you have space for your own thoughts about the notes you take in the larger area. In addition, you may wish to provide headings for the two parts—"Summary" and "Reaction," or "Notes" and "Comments," for example.

Both the Cornell method and the double-column notebook can be used for taking notes in class and for taking notes while you read. You may wish, however, to use the Cornell method for in-class notes and the double-column notebook for your reading and study notes, or a combination of the techniques if you prefer to have only one set of notes for a course. Whichever method you use and however you use it, try to take advantage of the opportunities for thinking each provides. If you do, you will find yourself "making" notes and not just "taking" them. And you may also find yourself making notes about your questions and comments as well.

Double-Column Notebook Example

Here is an example of the double-column notebook based on a passage from an essay by Katherine Anne Porter. Notice how one side summarizes the writer's idea, interpreting what she is saying; and notice how the other side raises questions, offers judgments, and makes connections with other things.

Adventure is sometimes fun, but not too often. Not if you can remember what really happened; all of it. It passes, seems to lead nowhere much, is something to tell friends to amuse them, maybe. "Once upon a time," I can hear myself saying, for I once said it, "I scaled a cliff in Boulder, Colorado, with my bare hands, and in Indian moccasins, bare-legged. And at nearly the top, after six hours of feeling for toe- and fingerholds, and the gayest feeling in the world that when I got to the top I should see something wonderful, something that sounded awfully like a bear growled out of a cave, and I scuttled down out of there in a hurry." This is a fact. I had never climbed a mountain in my life, never had the least wish to climb one. But there I was, for perfectly good reasons, in a hut on a mountainside in heavenly sunny though sometimes stormy weather, so I went out one morning and scaled a very minor cliff; alone, unsuitably clad, in the season when rattlesnakes are casting their skins; and if it was not a bear in that cave, it was some kind of unfriendly animal who growls at people; and this ridiculous escapade, which was nearly six hours of the hardest work I ever did in my life, toeholds and fingerholds on a cliff, put me to bed for just nine days with a complaint the local people called "muscle poisoning." I don't know exactly what they meant, but I do remember clearly that I could not turn over in bed without help and in great agony. And did it teach me anything? I think not, for three years later I was climbing a volcano in Mexico, that celebrated unpronounceably named volcano, Popocatepetl, which everybody who comes near it climbs sooner or later; but was that any reason for me to climb it? No. And I was knocked out for weeks, and that finally did teach me: I am not supposed to go climbing things. Why did I not know in the first place? For me, this sort of thing must come under the head of Adventure.

I think it is pastime of rather an inferior sort, yet I have heard men tell yarns like this only a very little better: their mountains were higher, or their sea was wider, or their bear was bigger and noisier, or their cliff was steeper and taller, yet there was no point whatever to any of it except that it had happened. This is not enough. May it not be, perhaps, that experience, that is, the thing that happens to a person living from day to day, is anything at all that sinks in? is, without making any claims, a part of your growing and changing life? what it is that happens in your mind, your heart?

Source: "St. Augustine and the Bullfight," Katherine Anne Porter

Example of Double-Column Notebook

Summary	Comments
Porter argues that adventure is not very much fun, not much of it, and not most of the time. She criticizes her mountain-climbing experience by saying that she didn't learn anything from it and that it caused physical pain.	Perhaps she means that adventures provide only the illusion of fun. They are not fun when they occur; we make them fun only in retrospect. After all we invested time, money, energy, etc. in "having" those adventures.
Porter adds a twist: that many people's adventures do not really differ from hers. She suggests that the differences are of <u>degree</u> rather than of <u>kind</u>.	Her tone here is strongly condemnatory. Is she fair in reducing adventure to "climbing things"? My adventures, good and bad, involve more than this.
Adventure is only what <u>happens</u>, not what the happening <u>means</u>. For Porter, adventure alone is never enough. That is, adventure is only an external experience, which Porter distinguishes from <u>real</u> experience, what happens <u>after</u> the adventure is over.	Her tone at times seems hesitant, questioning, as if she is thinking things out rather than insisting on her views. Yet she seems to believe what she is saying. Is this part of her persuasive strategy?
This real experience is not physical but intellectual and emotional.	Her concern with <u>real</u> experience links up with the idea that wisdom and maturity derive from reflecting on what happens to us.

Example of Double-Column Notebook

Summary	Comments
Experience for Porter changes the mind and affects the heart and spirit. But adventure changes nothing— though it is the raw material which can be converted to real experience.	If this is the case, then isn't Porter being somewhat hard on <u>mere</u> adventure? If she converts adventure into *real* experience, hasn't she then redeemed adventure after all?
Experience is a way of seeing a kind of perspective that leads to under-standing.	Compare Porter's idea with Annie Dillard's on "Seeing" from <u>Pilgrim at Tinker Creek</u>?

Exercise 6-2

Try out the Cornell system and the double-column notebook technique for a few of your classes and for some reading assignments as well.

Consider which method works best for you. Perhaps one method is better suited to some of your classes while another method is more useful for your other classes.

The Cornell and double-column notebook techniques can be supplemented by other notetaking strategies, such as underlining, highlighting, annotating, and outlining.

Underlining and Highlighting

One simple technique for taking notes on your reading outside class is to underline or highlight key passages. An alternative is to put a system of checkmarks or symbols in the margin of your text. In reviewing your text later, you can quickly reread the marked, underlined, or highlighted sections. (Be careful, though, not to underline or highlight too much—10 to 15 percent would be a lot.)

You may wish in fact to devise a slightly more coded system. For example, you may wish to underline important factual passages and highlight those containing important ideas. Or you may wish to highlight passages of extra importance and underline those of lesser but still some importance. Or you may wish to use a single check for passages to reread, a double check for those to study, and a triple check (or a +) for the most important passages of all. The main thing is to do something to your text that will make it easier to review efficiently later. Don't forget to identify on first use the meaning of any abbreviations or symbols you employ.

Annotating

You can go beyond underlining, highlighting, and checking by putting brief annotations or notes in the margins. These marginal notations may be questions, reactions, objections, or symbols such as ?? to indicate places where the text confuses you.

Annotations provide another convenient way to become engaged in texts you are reading or studying. When you are annotating a text, you are actively responding to it, thinking about it, and putting yourself in a good position to understand it. Annotating texts as preparation for class discussion will also help you find your way quickly to points you wish to make or questions you wish to raise in class discussion.

Here is a passage with accompanying annotations.

Do men dominate women in conversation?

It's almost a truism that interrupting others is a way of dominating them. It is rare to find an article on gender and language that does not make this claim. Tellingly, however, linguists Deborah James and Sandra Clarke reviewed all the research they could find on gender and interruption and did not find a clear pattern of males interrupting females. Especially surprising was their conclusion that the studies that investigated how much interruption took place in all-female as compared to all-male conversations actually found more interruption, not less, in all-female groups. James and Clarke note that in order to understand this pattern, it is necessary to ask what the speakers are *doing* when they talk over other speakers. Does the interruption show support for the other speaker, or does it contradict or change the topic? Overlapping talk can be a way of exerting status or establishing connection. (I prefer to use the term "overlap" to avoid the interpretation—and accusation— implicit in the term "interruption.")

females interrupt each other more than males

inter- ruption & rapport

Some speakers consider talking along with another to be a show of enthusiastic participation in the conversation, creating connections; others assume that only one voice should be heard at a time, so for them any overlap is an interruption, an attempt to wrest the floor, a power play. The result of this difference is that enthusiastic listeners who talk along to establish rapport can be perceived by

inter- ruption & control

others as interrupting—and are furthermore blamed for bad intentions: trying to "dominate" the conversation.

overlap is neutral

The key to whether an overlap (something neutral) becomes an interruption (something negative) depends on whether or not there is symmetry, or balance. If one speaker repeatedly overlaps and another repeatedly gives way, the resulting communication is unbalanced, and the effect (though not necessarily the intent) is domination. But if both speakers avoid overlap, or if both speakers overlap each other and win out equally, there is symmetry and no domination, regardless of speakers' intentions. The very engagement in a symmetrical struggle for the floor can be experienced as creating rapport, in the spirit of ritual opposition analogous to sports. Further, an imbalance can result from differences in the purpose for which overlap is used. If one speaker chimes in to show support, and the other cuts in to take the floor, the floor-taking overlapper will tend to dominate by determining the topics and expressing more ideas and opinions.

balance and imbalance in conversations

analogy with sports "ritual" opposition?

context

To know whether an overlap is an interruption, you must consider the context (for example, cooperative overlapping is more likely to occur in casual conversation among friends than in a job interview), speakers' habitual styles (ovelaps are more likely not to be interruptions among those with a style I call "high-involvement"), and the interaction of their styles (an interruption is more likely to result between speakers whose styles differ with regard to pausing and overlap). This is not to say that one cannot use interruption to dominate a conversation or a person, but only that overlap is not always intended as an interruption and an attempt to dominate.   *

the main point

Outlining

An additional technique for taking notes on important material is to outline a class lecture or a chapter from one of your textbooks.

Outlining is especially helpful in giving you an overview of a lecture or section of a text. In lecture courses, whose instructors organize their material well, you will find outlining both easy and useful. On occasions, when you do not have the time or the need to do more elaborate kinds of notetaking, outlining can serve as an efficient way to keep you focused on what you are reading.

Here is a sample outline for the passage previously annotated.

Conversational Interrupting and Dominance

I. Does interruption indicate a desire to dominate a conversation?
   A. Many studies on gender conversations say yes.
   B. James and Clarke say no.

II. What else does conversational interruption indicate?
   A. It shows support for the speaker.
      1. It suggests enthusiastic participation.
      2. It creates connections.
   B. It contradicts the speaker.
   C. It changes the topic.
      1. It shifts power.
      2. It establishes dominance.

III. What problems occur with interruptions in conversation?
   A. Misunderstanding is one major problem.
      1. Conversational imbalance occurs.
      2. Enthusiasm is perceived as domineering.
   B. Dominance is a second significant problem.

IV. Is context important in conversation?
   A. Formal and casual conversations require contexts.
   B. High- and low-involvement conversation styles reflect differing contexts.

Some Final Suggestions for Notetaking

Here are a few additional things you can do to make effective use of your notes.

1. *Organize* both your class and your reading notes. At the very least, use separate notebooks (or sections of a looseleaf binder) for different courses.

2. *Label* and *date* your notes. The date will tell you at what point in a course you covered specific material. The label will help you quickly locate topics you may wish to review.

3. *Edit* and *revise* your notes. Go through your notes periodically (especially your class notes) to make handwriting legible, to fill in missing words, to add details, and to make connections with further points you have learned from the time you first took the notes. (You may wish to add the later notes in a different color ink.)

4. *Separate* your comments and observations from the ideas of your instructor and from the authors of the texts you read. If you wish to use your notes in a paper or other written assignment, you will have an easy time identifying your own ideas—as long as you separate or otherwise distinguish them.

Exercise 6-3

Select one of the strategies from the preceding list and apply it to the notes for two of your courses.

Improving Study Skills

As you already know, study skills are intimately related to notetaking skills. The advice given earlier in this chapter on taking notes outside of class provides one approach to improving your study skills. Some additional aspects of studying include the following topics:

1. Finding an appropriate place to study
2. Mapping out a schedule of study time
3. Setting goals for study sessions
4. Learning to focus and concentrate
5. Increasing your understanding of what you study
6. Remembering what you study

Finding a Suitable Study Environment

Some students swear that they study best in bed—prone or propped up by pillows. For most, however, this place and position is an invitation to study disaster. Your body "knows" when it is in bed, and prepares itself for sleeping rather than studying. Better than your bed is a desk or table with ample room for you to spread out your books, papers, notes, and other materials. You might set yourself up at a library desk or table, in a room in your home or in a campus residence hall—as long as the place allows you to work without distractions.

A hard chair with a straight back is probably best for most people since you can't get overly comfortable in such a chair. Any kind of chair will do, however, as long as it is not so comfortable you feel like sitting back and resting in it. Sitting on the edge of your chair and leaning slightly forward over your books is recommended, since that posture keeps you active and alert.

Taking Stock

Where do you prefer to study? Why? What are the good and bad features of your study site? When you can't study in your favorite environment, where do you study? When do you do your best studying? Why? What do you use as a secondary back-up time to do your regular studying?

You should study in a place free of distractions—no radio blaring, no MTV, no friends stopping by to chat, no children seeking attention. And it should also be well enough lit for you to read comfortably.

Mapping Out a Schedule of Study Time

As important as an appropriate place to study is adequate time. Ideally, you should try to study at times when you are most alert and work your best. Some people work best early in the day, others work better late at night. Whatever your optimum study time is, try to ensure that you schedule your study hours for that time. Most important is that you study your most difficult and demanding subjects during your optimum study times. You should also study those subjects first, while your mind is at its best.

But reality may interfere with your ideal study schedule. When circumstances prevent you from studying during your optimum time, you need to have other regularly scheduled study. Managing your time is an issue unto itself, but allocating sufficient time to prepare for classes, review your notes, complete reading and writing assignments, and study for quizzes, tests, and exams is crucial for academic success.

Setting Goals for Studying

Whether you are settling in for a long study session for a major exam or just squeezing in a short period to review for a quiz, you should have a specific goal for your study session. Before you get down to work, you need to have an idea of what you want to accomplish and how long you plan on studying to reach your goal.

For long study sessions, you should set small goals with shorter time periods within your overall session and overall goal. If, for example, you need to review three chapters for a midterm during a single study session, you should break up your study period into three blocks of time and set a specific goal for each. When you start or finish your second study session on this material, you should also briefly review the main points of the first session. For the third session, do a quick review of the main points you studied in the first two sessions. Three short 1-hour sessions are preferable to one marathon 3-hour session. The shorter sessions give you a chance to review and reinforce what you learn. You will also be less apt to tire and can thus retain more of what you learn.

Exercise 6-4

Set up a study schedule for an upcoming test. Break down your study time into manageable blocks of time (roughly 1 hour each). Identify a specific goal you want to accomplish for each hour of study.

Taking Breaks

To make efficient use of your time, it is necessary to take breaks from concentrated periods of study. This is so because there are limits to how long we can concentrate, just as there are limits to how many things we can hold at once in our short-term memory. In a 2-hour study session, for example, you may need one break after 50 or 55 minutes. In a 3-hour session, you might schedule two breaks, one per hour. A brief 5-minute break will allow you to relax and then return to concentrate better than you would have without taking the break. To avoid stretching breaks beyond 5, or perhaps 10 minutes, you can use a kitchen timer or a watch or radio alarm.

Exercise 6-5

During your next study session, schedule breaks at predetermined intervals. Force yourself to take the breaks even if you are not accustomed to doing so. Then assess whether the breaks increased your concentration during the time immediately after them.

Dealing with Disturbances

To complete assignments on time, to do necessary studying on schedule, and generally to keep abreast of your academic work, you will need to minimize distractions. Insist upon some time when your friends and family may not disturb you.

If you have an important exam to prepare for, a major project or paper to complete, you will need to find or make some uninterrupted time to do your work. Don't be afraid to put a "Do Not Disturb" sign on your door. Your roommate, spouse, children, friends—whoever—will simply have to realize that there will be times when they can best show their support by letting you do your work undisturbed. If this doesn't work, find a secluded place where they can't find you so you can do a few hours of uninterrupted studying. The library provides quiet space for this purpose.

To gain that disturbance-free time, you will probably have to make trade-offs. If you need 2 hours to study or work, ask your spouse to take care of the kids for that time and do something in return later. If you are the only one available to care for the children, make a deal with them to gain the time you need. Rent educational films for them, promise them a special treat. Make a game or contest of "Mommy's (or "Daddy's") study time." Or find some way to include them. You will have opportunities later to do something in return when you have free time.

It's difficult to juggle schedules and balance your responsibilities for others with your academic obligations. You will need to be realistic about how much you can do. Be reasonable in assessing what you can accomplish. If you find you've tried to do too much, cut back where you can and plan more reasonably in the future. If your courseload is too heavy, speak with an academic counselor or an advisor, and discuss your situation with some of your more understanding professors to consider your options.

And don't be afraid to say "no" to demands on your time when your schedule is crowded.

Exercise 6-6

Talk with your classmates, roommates, family, or friends about ways to ensure that you have some disturbance-free time for important academic projects. Brainstorm with other students about ways to handle unwanted interruptions such as noise, phone calls, uninvited conversations, and temptations to become involved in other activities. See how they resolve such situations.

Learning To Concentrate

Having a study schedule and setting goals to achieve them will not be of much use unless you can concentrate and focus your intellectual energy on your study tasks. To concentrate means to zero in on what you wish to read, learn, think about. To do that, you need to find ways to shut out distractions both external and internal.

Taking Stock

Think back over your last two or three study sessions, long or short. How long did you study before taking a break? Did you reward yourself for your efforts? Why or why not?

Essential for concentration is a quiet environment and one in which you have everything you need to do your work. Beyond external quiet, you may need to make an effort to shut out distracting thoughts and create internal quiet. Try to become absorbed in the details of your work and try to avoid giving in to distracting thoughts of what you'll be doing later. When you catch yourself daydreaming or thinking about something other than the task, stop yourself and direct your mind and body back to your work.

It is also essential to have adequate rest and enough to eat. Eating too much before studying, however, can make you both physically and intellectually sluggish. You will probably do better with a small edge on your appetite.

The guidelines for active studying provided earlier, such as annotating, highlighting, underlining, and outlining, your texts, will also help in sustaining your concentration. Also, try to avoid studying for long periods (more than an hour) without taking a break. A 5- to 10-minute break every hour will enhance your ability to concentrate.

Another strategy you can use to keep focused is to promise yourself a reward at the end of your study session. If you have planned to study for an entire afternoon, give yourself the evening off. Or if you have met your study goals, treat yourself to a favorite food, a TV show, or a movie with friends. The lure of the well-earned reward will help keep you studying.

Improving Understanding

The study techniques presented are designed both to help you meet your study goals and to help you learn, whether your goal is to understand sonata form, the chemistry of ionic bonds, the gross national product, or the anatomy and physiology of the human digestive system.

The following strategies for studying can enhance your understanding of course materials.

1. *Translate* into your own words what you recorded from your instructor in class or what you copied from a textbook. Putting another's idea into your words helps you to clarify your understanding and can make you aware of what you do not understand. When you are able to translate a concept into your own words by paraphrasing or summarizing it, you demonstrate to yourself that you really do understand it.

2. *Convert* words you read or heard into diagrams or pictures that illustrate the idea or process described. Sometimes it is helpful to come at a concept from a different perspective. Visualizing a process by representing it in a diagram and labeling its parts or stages not only helps you "see" it better, but also helps you remember the process.

3. *Associate* what you are learning with what you already know. Link the new and unfamiliar with old and familiar knowledge. All learning, essentially, involves connecting what you don't know with what you do. In fact, if you cannot relate new information and new ideas to what you already know, you won't really learn them or remember them—that is, you won't be able to use the new ideas and information until you can relate them to what you have already learned.

4. *Preview* what you are studying when you start (a chapter of a textbook, for example). Previewing a text involves looking it over quickly before diving in deeply and reading and studying it carefully. Previewing gives you a chance to survey the text overall. You can see where it starts, where it ends, and what ground it covers in between. You can also gain an overview of how one part of the overall text for study relates to other parts.

5. *Review* quickly when you finish studying. A brief review of what you cover during an entire study session helps you do two things: see relationships among parts of the material; and solidify and reinforce what you learned as you focused on the individual parts. Review is an essential part of the study process. Moreover, reviewing should be a regular part of your study habit, whether you are memorizing foreign language vocabulary for a minor quiz or learning economic models for a major exam. Your review-study should also be done regularly—daily or at least a few times a week, and then weekly or biweekly for larger chunks of material, and, finally, monthly and quarterly in preparation for major tests.

Exercise 6-7

For an upcoming test apply the steps presented in this section: translate, convert, associate, preview, and review. Spend some additional time working with your notes, your textbook, and your class materials. Set aside enough time to prepare adequately.

Remembering What You Have Studied

The first principle of remembering what you have studied is simple: *You cannot remember what you have not learned.*

The second principle is: *Be selective.* You will not be able to remember everything. As a result, you will have to make decisions about what to memorize and what to learn but not learn by heart.

The third principle is: *Associate what you are learning with what you already know.*

You can also apply some time-honored techniques to help you remember details. Here are two useful ones:

1. *Mnemonics.* Mnemonics are memory aids that help you remember things by linking them in an easy-to-remember way. You may have learned how many days are in each of the months of the year by the following rhyme:

Thirty days hath September,
April, June, and November.
February has twenty-eight.
All the rest have thirty-one.

You probably learned the colors and their order in the spectrum with the mnemonic name *Roy G. Biv* for red, orange, yellow, green, blue, indigo, and violet. Or you may have used the word *homes* as a mnemonic for the names of the five great lakes: Huron, Ontario, Michigan, Erie, and Superior.

Try to create your own mnemonics for lists and groups of details you need to memorize for your courses.

2. *Acronyms.* An acronym is a word made up of the first letters of a series of words. MADD, for example, is an acronym for Mothers Against Drunk Driving, and NAFTA is an acronym for North American Free Trade Agreement. But IBM (International Business Machines) and BCCI (Bank of Credit and Commerce International) are not, since the letters, while forming an abbreviation, do not make up a word. You may wish to create your own acronyms to help you remember sets of details or key concepts in some of your courses. In a philosophy course, for example, you might use the acronym SPA to remember the order of birth and influence of the Greek philosophers Socrates, Plato, and Aristotle.

Remember that to study effectively you need to approach your study sessions in a proper frame of mind. You need to set a goal and want to achieve it in the time you have available.

Chapter 7

Taking Quizzes, Tests, and Examinations

Chapter Highlights

Tests are a part of life and a significant part of college life. This chapter describes different kinds of tests and how to prepare for them effectively. It examines practical test-taking strategies and includes the following topics:

- Gauging different kinds of tests
- Studying effectively for tests
- Writing under the pressure of time
- Using long- and short-term test preparation strategies

Key Questions

Take a minute to think about the following key questions.

1. Do you become anxious before or during tests? Some kinds of tests? Tests in certain subjects?

2. How do you usually prepare for tests? For tests in English? In history and the social sciences? In the natural sciences? In your major?

3. Do you perform better on short-answer tests, essay, fill-in-the-blank, or multiple-choice tests? Do you know why?

4. What can you do to perform better on tests?

Tests: What They Are

Since your grades and academic profile throughout your academic career are tied to being tested, it makes sense to learn how to perform well on examinations. Doing well on tests depends on being well prepared for them.

This is not news to you. After all, no one who goes through a dozen years of school tests and takes standardized tests for college admission is unfamiliar with the importance of tests. What may be new, however, is the notion that you can use specific techniques and strategies to improve your performance. Your improved performance will reflect enhanced understanding and greater learning. In short, your higher test scores will reflect your stronger grasp of the subjects you are being tested on.

Let's start by considering what tests are and how instructors use them.

The most familiar academic meaning of the term *test* is a set of questions that, when answered, demonstrates how much or how little you know about a subject. A test may measure how well you have absorbed and understood an instructor's presentation of a subject. Depending on the nature of the test, however, and depending upon your skill in taking tests, your performance on any one test may not reflect the range of your knowledge or the depth of your understanding. Following the advice in this chapter will greatly increase the likelihood that your test grades will reflect what you know and how well you understand it.

Why Do Teachers Give Tests?

One reason has already been suggested: to see how much students have learned. Another is to enable teachers to assign grades. Still another is to see how well teachers are conveying an understanding of the subject to their students. Tests can provide measures of instructors' success as well as the success of their students. Finally, instructors may use tests to teach something new rather than simply to measure what has already been learned. Such tests typically challenge students to push beyond what they already know and to apply their knowledge. Tests can assess learning, measure teaching effectiveness, and also teach.

It's important to realize that more than one purpose may govern the tests you take in college. It is important to be aware when tests are being given, what kinds of tests your instructors will give, and how much any one test counts toward your final grade. It is also important to know which of your instructors construct their own tests and which may use readymade tests that accompany your textbooks. Some departments may standardize tests for all sections of particular courses. The more you know about the testing done in your courses and sections, the better you will be able to prepare for them intelligently.

Kinds of Tests

It's certainly not true that "a test is a test is a test." A quiz is not a test, and a test is not an exam—unless your instructor says so. Be sure that whatever language your instructors use to describe their ways of measuring your understanding, you are clear about how important any one test is for your overall course grade, for learning, and for accomplishing specific goals—whether your own or your instructor's.

Typically, instructors make broad distinctions between quizzes and tests and between tests and exams. Let's begin with quizzes.

Assessing Quizzes

Under normal circumstances a quiz is brief and covers a small amount of material, perhaps the reading for a single class. Instructors give quizzes to encourage students to prepare for class. They also give quizzes to stimulate class discussion or to ensure attendance. And they quiz students to preview various kinds of questions that will appear on midterm tests and final exams.

Be clear about how much weight an instructor assigns to his or her quizzes. In some classes quizzes may add up to a significant portion of the grade—perhaps as much as a third or more. The important thing is to know the value assigned to quizzes.

You should also know whether quizzes will be announced. And if you miss a quiz, you should know whether there will be a penalty, whether you will need to take a make-up quiz, or whether you may be allowed a certain number of missed quizzes. Sometimes instructors who rely heavily on quizzes will allow students to miss a few without penalty. For example, an instructor may give twelve quizzes over a quarter or half a term and count ten of them. If you miss two, the ten you take count. If, on the other hand, you take all twelve, the two graded lowest may be dropped.

Instructors may also use quizzes as a way to help you identify weaknesses in your understanding. Quizzes provide feedback about how well students understand course material. If you do poorly on some quizzes but compensate on the more heavily weighted quarterly or midterm tests, your quiz grades may not be harmful to your final grade. Some instructors may even eliminate your quiz grades from the computation of your final grade. Since there is no single way instructors use quizzes, you should find out in every case how quizzes will be used, graded, and weighted in determining your final grade.

Taking Stock

Look over your course syllabi and take stock of the number and types of quizzes you will have in each course. Note how much each quiz counts towards the course grade. What are the teachers' purposes and goals in giving quizzes? What are your goals in preparing for them in different courses?

Considering Tests

Besides quizzes, you can expect, at strategic points in your courses, occasional longer and more heavily weighted tests. Many instructors divide the semester into quarters and test at the one-quarter, midpoint, three-quarter point, and end. Others may test a bit more frequently. Still others will test only at midterm and finals time. The general rule is that the less frequently tests are given, the more they count. But don't make the assumption that just because an instructor gives two or three tests in a term, those tests will be equally weighted. Ask.

Ask, too, about the kinds of tests your instructors give. Some will give only multiple-choice or short-answer tests. Others will test only through extended written responses to essay questions, some of which may include or require a "take-home" option. Still other instructors use only demonstrations or some form of applied learning.

Suppose that a quarterly test is being given in your introductory psychology course. You have been reading works by Sigmund Freud, Melanie Klein, C. G. Jung, Anna Freud, and Karen Horney. It will help you greatly in your reading and notetaking to know whether you should be prepared to write essays that compare and contrast or classify their theories—about dreams, symbols, sexuality, or something else. Your instructors may tell you how long the test will take and what percentage of time you should devote to essays and to short-answer responses. They will usually also indicate the value of each part of the test. If they don't, you should ask.

Analyzing Exams

Examinations. Exams. Finals. Dreaded words for the unprepared. A chance to shine or to redeem yourself if you are well prepared.

Final exams count heavily. The word *final* has a sense of seriousness, even "finality," about it. After the final exam you have no additional chance to prove yourself. There will be no recourse, and thus finals are critical to your grades.

What should you know about final exams? Essentially, it is the same as what you need to know about other tests. Here are a few things to consider.

- How much does it count in computing your final grade? One-third? Half? More?
- How much does it cover? From the midpoint on? The work of the entire course? (In the second case, the final is "cumulative.")
- What kind of final exam can you expect? Part short answer and part essay? If so, how much time will be allotted for each section and how much will each count toward computing your exam grade?
- Will the final exam differ in its structure or in the kinds of questions it includes from other tests given in the course?
- How difficult an exam can you expect? Do you have any basis for comparison with exams or tests from prior years?

This last question can be answered partly by looking at earlier tests for the course. But you can also get a sense by listening carefully to what the instructor may say about the final exam.

Exercise 7-1

Talk with two of your instructors about the kinds of tests they give. Ask them why they give tests, how they grade them, and what they think might happen if students were not tested.

Preparing for Tests and Exams

Preparing for tests and exams begins with preparing for class. It should not end there, but that is where it should certainly begin. Otherwise you will jeopardize your chances for success. You can also set yourself a study schedule as an important test or exam approaches, including last-minute study. We can speak, then, of long-term and short-term test preparation.

Long-term Test Preparation

Your long-term preparation for tests and exams includes faithful class attendance, careful class preparation, thoughtful participation, reviewing, and notetaking both in class and out. Long-term test preparation should include compensating for missed classes by talking with your instructors and by copying notes of a classmate whose academic performance and abilities you respect. Further, long-term preparation may involve establishing a study group that meets regularly throughout the term (not just the night before a major exam) to discuss class lectures and meetings, review assigned readings, compare notes, and do short-term test preparation.

Your long-term preparation essentially includes everything you can and should do in taking the course seriously.

You can begin your long-term test preparation by attending class meetings conscientiously and participating in them actively. The obvious reasons for attending class are not the only reasons. Of course you should attend to learn whatever the instructor has to teach. And you should attend to ensure that you understand what's required for assignments. But attendance is important for other reasons as well. Instructors know who is present and who cuts. You do not ingratiate yourself with teachers when you brazenly and frequently cut their classes. In doing so, you send the message that you don't care about the course very much, or you don't think you are learning anything worthwhile. You also intimate that the class doesn't merit your efforts. And further, you suggest that you can learn what's necessary without the instructor's assistance.

Even when a course tries your patience and you can barely sustain your attention, you need to make the effort, if only because it will affect your performance and your final grade. You may think that studying the text or doing the readings is enough, whether that text is on business law or whether those readings include a series of twentieth-century novels. To some extent, you are right; you can learn a lot on your own. No one would quarrel with that, probably not even the instructors whose classes you are tempted to cut.

Attending class gives you an extra chance to understand, along with an additional forum for developing your understanding. If you can learn a lot on your own, you can also bring that knowledge to the classroom and use it to stimulate discussion or to invite the instructor to move beyond the routine work for the day. And showing up for class also allows you to share your thoughts with other students. This is important since you will learn from other students as well as from your books and your instructors.

You can make a favorable impression by showing that you are a serious student, one who cares enough to prepare thoughtfully and is courteous enough to attend class attentively. Even though impressions may not be the most important thing, they do count. Try to make those impressions good ones.

Taking Stock

Review your attitude to class attendance. How often do you miss class? Why? What do you do when you miss class? If you have not already done so, get the phone number of two students you can call when you miss a class.

Being Prepared for Class

It is not enough merely to attend class, necessary as that is. You also need to demonstrate seriousness and diligence, and you must show commitment to the instructor's educational program for the course. To do that, prepare. Has a book been assigned for discussion? Read it. Is a quiz being given? Study for it. Is a writing assignment due? Turn it in—on time. Little things, you may say. Perhaps. But a lot of little things accumulate to make a big impression. They contribute not only toward your final grade, but also toward the thoroughness and solidity of your understanding and learning. And because some courses build foundations for others, maintaining class attendance, developing thoughtful study habits, and securing favorable faculty impressions will benefit you in many courses.

Each little thing you do for a course, each paper you write, each assignment you read, each class you attend, contributes toward your sense of security and confidence with the course material. You'll know more of what's being taught. And you'll also realize when you don't understand something. If you miss classes, and if you defer or otherwise avoid doing assignments, you may think you know more than you actually do. And when a test is scheduled, you may be less secure with the course material than you should be.

Ideally, your long-term preparation should include reading and doing assignments before the class meets, attending class regularly, and following up with additional study and review. To succeed in test preparation, you need to take your work seriously, make a study schedule, and stick to it.

Exercise 7-2

Look back at a recent test on which you performed well and one on which you performed poorly (or at least not as well). Analyze what enabled you to excel on the test or why you didn't do well. Consider what you could to do to improve your performance.

Short-Term Test Preparation

Depending on how successful your long-term preparation has been and on how comfortable and confident you are with the course material, your short-term preparation can vary widely. For a course in which you have been doing the work commendably all along, you may need no more than a once over lightly—perhaps a couple hours for review.

For a course in which you feel unsure and unsettled, even if you have been relatively studious all along, you should devote more time, partly because the added time and effort will increase your confidence, and partly because it will enhance your familiarity with the material.

For occasions when you have a few days to a week or so to study, you should block out three or four study periods during times when you concentrate and work best. Schedule these sessions to avoid conflicting with class meetings in other subjects and with other things you either need to do or want to do.

If there is a hockey game you simply must watch or a party you've been waiting for anxiously, schedule your study time before it. In fact, it's a good idea to study hard early on a day you will have something exciting to look forward to later. If you study hard beforehand, you can watch the game or attend the mixer feeling that you've earned the right to enjoy yourself. The alternative might be that you'll feel guilty either during the activity or afterward because you've neglected your academic responsibilities.

Scheduling Study Time

Blocking out time for study is essential if you are to have a reasonable chance to be well prepared for classes and exams.

Let's say you've blocked out three study sessions, one 2 hours, the others 4 hours each. That's a total of 10 hours—though about 10 percent of that time you will take short breaks. That leaves you with 9 hours of study time.

Next, you should break up your 2-hour study block into two 1-hour chunks. Do the same for your 4-hour blocks, first cutting them in half, and then in half again. For each of the major blocks (2-hour and 4-hour) decide what you want to cover and how much you can reasonably accomplish. Do the same for the smaller one-hour blocks.

Then assess what you need to do in preparing for a test. How much time for reading or rereading the text? How much for reviewing your notes? How much for memorizing? How much for writing additional notes or for trying some hypothetical questions? Allow time for getting help with material you don't understand and for questions that come up while studying. And allow time, too, for building breaks into your study schedule. Just remember to remain conscientious and disciplined enough to return to diligent study after those breaks.

If you feel confident that you have all the time you need, you should then set to work. If, on the other hand, you know that you'll need additional time, you'll have to make that time somehow, perhaps by getting up earlier a few days, perhaps missing one of your planned activities. But let's be optimistic and say that your original schedule will be enough.

Taking Stock

For a major test you have this term, do a time analysis. Estimate realistically how much time you will need to study—how much to learn new material, how much to review familiar material, how much for reading and thinking, for writing and notetaking. Block out chunks of study time and label them with general headings for study—chapter groups or topics, for example. Then break the time chunks in half and divide your topics further.

Exercise 7-3

Prepare a study chart for a major test two or three weeks away. Include both large and small blocks of study time. Break down any large blocks you include into smaller segments. In each segment, identify specific tasks, goals, or topics.

Studying for Tests and Exams

Here are some things you need to think about when you study for a test. Making sensible choices about each of them will enable you to use your study time effectively.

- Your environment
- Your time
- Your goals
- Your rewards
- Your tools

Let's take these up briefly one at a time.

First, *environment.* Find a comfortable place to study—but not so comfortable that you find yourself lounging or dozing. Wherever you study best (your dorm room, the library, a vacant classroom, your kitchen, dining room, bedroom) make sure the temperature is right. Hot, stuffy rooms may put you to sleep. Cold ones may keep you from concentrating.

If you concentrate best at a desk, make sure that's where you seat yourself. If you need room to write, be sure you have it. Wherever you end up, make sure you won't be distracted by music, by other students or family members, or by other temptations to keep you from your work—unless music helps you study better or other people encourage you or answer your questions. Of course, some of this advice may be impossible for you to follow—at least some of the time. But do your best to find some disturbance-free space.

Second, *time.* If you study best in the morning, don't schedule your heaviest exam prep time for late at night. If you're a night owl, then set yourself up for late night study. You know your own work rhythm. Arrange your time so you can work at your highest level of efficiency and productivity.

Third, *goals.* Set goals for your study sessions. Try to accomplish something specific at each session. Plan to outline a chapter or to memorize a set of formulas, or work a set number of sample problems. Plan to review your class notes or to reread and take new notes on a specific number of pages or chapters. If your overall goal for the session is ambitious, cut it into several smaller segments. (Avoid marathon study sessions.) Tackle your smaller goals one at a time. It sounds simple, and it is—as long as you work on one thing at a time. Rather than fretting at the number of study hours ahead of you or the magnitude of your task, divide everything into manageable units and work on the small pieces. Before long, they'll add up. You'll find yourself developing momentum.

Fourth, *rewards.* Periodically, after accomplishing one of your goals, reward yourself. Take an ice-cream break. Chat for a few minutes with friends. Read an article in a popular magazine. But be strict with yourself. Set a limit for your break; then return to work.

After you meet some of your longer, more ambitious goals, take a few hours off to watch a ball game or see a movie. Do some exercise or treat yourself to a special dinner. If you've worked hard before the pleasurable activity, you'll feel as if you deserve it.

Fifth, keep your study *tools* handy. You'll need a watch, pen and paper, the necessary books. Consider doing some writing while you study. By writing I simply mean keeping a pen handy and using it from time to time. You can jot notes in the margins of your books. You can make a brief outline of what you've read. You can ask yourself questions that occur to you while you study. And you can make connections between what you are studying and what you remember from class discussion. If you are reviewing your notes, you can make additional notes in the margins or on facing pages of your notebook.

Exercise 7-4

Take an inventory of where, when, how long, and what materials you had with you during your last few major study sessions. Evaluate your study behavior according to the guidelines just given.

Taking Stock

Consider your previous experience with study groups. If the groups were successful, explain why; if unsuccessful, identify the probable reasons for the failure. Are you inclined to work again with a study group? For a particular course or exam? Why or why not?

Working with a Study Group

If you have the time and inclination, you may want to join a study group to prepare for a major test. The advantage of group study is that some members will see things that others don't. Some will have better notes, some will be better prepared, and some will be better able to anticipate the kinds of questions the instructor is likely to ask and possibly the kinds of responses likely to be considered strong.

The main danger of group study is that one or two students will dominate. They may direct the group's effort toward aspects of the course you either know very well already or think unimportant. Another danger is that the group will work inefficiently, wasting a lot of time in idle talk and socializing. Set an agenda; agree in advance how much time will be spent on each item and assign a person to keep track of time. Depending on your own learning style, you may prefer working with a group for an important test only if you have done so before, perhaps if you belong to a group that has met regularly throughout the term.

Recognize that there are differences in how people learn. You may learn best independently, or you may learn best as a member of a group. You may learn more efficiently and effectively as a subordinate in groups with a strong focus on task completion. Or you may learn better with a single tutor with whom you discuss key course issues or of whom you ask specific questions.

Memorizing

You may find it necessary to memorize facts and figures, formulas and sequences of events. Sometimes a major test is given with the assumption that you can remember many of the things you learned for earlier quizzes. If so, you'll need to review them and put them back into memory.

Useful rules exist for memorizing anything, whether you are learning it for the first time or whether you are relearning it.

1. *Focus.* Concentrate on what you are memorizing. If it's a piece of music, listen with your full attention. If it's a sequence of biochemical processes, look at the whole sequence and then break it into parts. Focus on those small parts.

Then put them back together. Analyze, or break the work down into small pieces. It's easier to memorize small elements than large ones. It's easier to memorize something large by building your way to the whole than by trying to swallow the whole thing in one mental gulp. You memorize a sonnet one line at a time until you have all fourteen lines stored in your memory.

2. *Associate.* Try to connect what you are memorizing with something else. You may recall learning the names of the lines of the musical staff (E-G-B-D-F) by associating those lines with the first letter of each word in this sentence: Every Good Boy Does Fine. You may have learned other things by means of rhyme.

3. *Repeat to reinforce.* Repetition is another useful technique for memorizing things. Ideally, you should memorize what you need to know early so you have time to reinforce it, thus impressing it more firmly in your mind when you review.

Reviewing to Remember

One of the best ways to remember what you learn in your study sessions is to review. You can use review three ways:

1. Review immediately after studying.
2. Repeat the review periodically—at the beginning of each study session.
3. Review cumulatively; that is, review the material from all previous study sessions at the beginning or end of each successive study session.

First, you should review immediately after you complete a study session. Ask yourself questions about the material, or have someone else ask you the questions. Note any questions you miss, and restudy the material.

Second, you can review again later after some time has elapsed. One technique is to review material from the previous study session at the beginning of the next one. In reviewing for a midterm exam, for instance, you might schedule four study sessions. You should review at the end of each session and at the beginning of the second, third, and last ones.

Third, you should review all the accumulated material at the beginning or end of each subsequent session. By the time you reach the fourth study session in preparing for a midterm or final exam, you will have reviewed the fourth chunk of material once, the third session chunk twice, the second session material three times, and the first session material four times.

Exercise 7-5

Select something to memorize. It can be something required for a course—verb conjugations, chemical formulas, the U.S. presidents. Or it can be something you'd like to memorize for yourself—the rules of chess, the lyrics of a song, the words of a famous speech. Apply the advice given in this chapter and memorize it.

Other Techniques for Aiding Memory

To remember something, you must want to remember it. Your intention is important. If you don't care about remembering a name, a date, a process, or a theory, you won't remember it. Think of how often you forget things you don't care about and remember what's important to you.

In deciding whether to intend to remember material for your courses, you must consider whether the material is important. Is it important enough to be checked on a test? Is it important enough in its own right—is it of immediate interest to you?

You will have more success in remembering course material when you organize and categorize what you learn. In learning to conjugate French verbs, study them in clusters or groups—*Er* and *Ir* verbs, for example. In learning about the history of philosophy, group philosophers according to whether they are Aristotelians, who begin with concrete sense experience, or Platonists, who begin with abstract ideas. You can group composers by their musical styles—Classical and Romantic, for example, or by their historical periods—medieval, Renaissance, Baroque, and so on.

Still other strategies to help you solidify and remember what you study include using more than one of your senses. Typically, you study silently, reading words on a page, perhaps hearing them soundlessly in your mind. You can try saying aloud what you want to remember. You can tape important information and play it back so you hear it. You can also walk around from time to time when you study, perhaps reciting aloud what you are trying to learn. The rhythm of your walking and the echo of your voice can lodge more deeply what you might study in silence.

Cramming

Cramming is an attempt to commit large amounts of information to memory in marathon study sessions. Cramming can overload your memory circuits so that you confuse things wildly. This confusion is especially likely if you are studying an unfamiliar subject with strange terminology, and you've let it go until a marathon cramming session. Such cramming is dangerous. At best, you will remember some things because they'll be fresh in your mind. At worst, you'll confuse what you've memorized, and you'll embarrass yourself. At most, even if you're reasonably successful and manage to avoid the pitfalls of cramming, how much will you actually remember? You may remember some

---

Taking Stock

Consider your experience with cramming—its benefits and drawbacks. Think about how you felt before, during, and after the cramming session. Think about how much you learned and how much you remembered later.

---

of what you study, but only for a short time. If you are really interested in learning, if you're concerned about real academic success, and if you want to develop your intellectual powers, you'll not cheat yourself by making cramming your primary method of study. In an emergency, as a last resort, for material you've already studied, it's all right. Otherwise it's not.

Guidelines for Taking Tests

A major test is sitting on your desk. What should you do? How should you proceed?

First, *collect yourself*. Don't let anxiety get the better of you. If you feel tense and nervous, breathe slowly and deeply for a few moments. Then spend a minute looking over the entire test to get a sense of the kinds of questions it contains. Make sure you know how much time you have overall and how much time you'll need for each part. Then set to work.

Second, *read the test instructions carefully*. Make sure you understand them. If you don't, ask for clarification.

Third, *be methodical* in approaching different kinds of questions.

If you are faced with multiple-choice questions, for example, consider each of the options presented. You will often be able to eliminate some answers immediately. Analyze those that remain, looking carefully at their differences and what those differences imply. If you are required to provide short answers, you should jot some key terms, concepts, phrases, and definitions on scrap paper for later use. Often the very act of writing down some of what you know will prompt you to recall other things you might block on at first.

A final note on short-answer tests. If a test is challenging enough, you will come across questions that stump you—at least initially. Rather than laboring over them, skip them and return to them after you have answered the ones you know. Try to get into a rhythm of responding correctly. Your confidence will pick up. And in the course of answering the questions you do know, you may find yourself recalling other details that help you respond accurately to those you had at first skipped. Try to go from general information to specific examples. You may find answers to earlier questions in those that come later.

True-False Questions

When taking true-false tests or sections of tests, mark first all the questions you are confident are either true or false. Consider those statements you are unsure about to be true unless you can find a reason to think them false. As a general rule, more statements are true on such tests than false. If you are not penalized for incorrect answers, and in situations where you must guess without a clue, guess true.

Be sure, however, in marking statements as true or false, that a statement is false if any part of it is false, or if it is only partly true. For example, the following statement is false because one part is false:

John F. Kennedy, Jimmy Carter, and Dwight D. Eisenhower were Democratic Presidents.

(Even though Kennedy and Carter were Democrats, Eisenhower was a Republican, falsifying the statement.)

Also, be leery of statements that lack qualifiers when you are answering true-false questions. Statements that include such words as *always, never, all,* and *none* are usually false. On the other hand, statements that include qualifying modifiers such as *sometimes, frequently, some,* and *many* tend more often to be true.

For example, the statement, "All college teachers give midterm and final exams," is false. The statement, "Many college teachers give midterm and final exams," is true. The difference in the statements is one small word (*many* instead of *all*), and it makes one big difference.

As a general rule, read true-false questions with extreme care. Look for single words that tip you off one way or the other about the statement's truth or falsity. You'll usually find them.

Multiple-Choice Questions

Multiple-choice questions are among the most difficult for students, largely because they often contain two apparently correct responses. Multiple-choice questions may be incomplete statements followed by different ways to complete them. They may also be complete statements or questions followed by a series of options for answers. Only one of the answer choices is considered correct or the best answer for the question.

In taking multiple-choice tests, you can use a few basic strategies.

First, answer the questions you are sure of first. Skip the more difficult ones, but come back to them after answering all that you are confident about.

Second, eliminate the answers you know are incorrect. If you can eliminate two answers in a question with four possible answers, you have a 50 percent chance of getting the question right even if you are unsure about the remaining answer options.

Third, before you decide on an answer, analyze the remaining answer possibilities as if they were true-false statements. Apply the techniques for analyzing true-false questions.

Fourth, look for an answer meaning "all of the above." Inclusive answers usually offer the best response. Consider this example:

Gold is used to make
a. jewelry
b. musical instruments
c. automobile equipment
d. all of the above

The correct answer is *d*. If you know that gold is used to make jewelry and musical instruments, your choice should be "all of the above" even if you don't know that gold is used to make some automobile equipment. Why? Because by answering *a*, you leave out musical instruments, which you know are sometimes made of gold. If you answer *b*, you leave out jewelry, which you also know exists.

Another type of inclusive answer for multiple-choice questions occurs in questions that do not include "all of the above" as an option. Consider the following example:

Height is likely to vary most among which of the following groups?
a. jockeys
b. basketball players
c. dentists
d. Pygmies

The most inclusive group of the four is dentists, who are not typically short, like jockeys and pygmies, or taller than average, like basketball players.

Other techniques for identifying correct multiple-choice options include being wary of extreme modifiers such as *always, never,* and *only*—just as when answering true-false questions. You should also not be seduced into selecting unfamiliar words when answering multiple-choice questions because test-makers often introduce strange terms as *distractors,* or incorrect answers.

On some occasions, however, when an unfamiliar term appears in a set of answers that contains others all of which you know are incorrect, you should choose the unfamiliar term as your answer. In that case, you would have eliminated the others as incorrect, with the unfamiliar term the only viable option.

Fill-in Questions

Fill-in questions require you to complete a statement by introducing words or phrases that you supply yourself. They are not given to you as a set of choices, as in true-false or multiple-choice questions.

To answer fill-in questions, you need to understand the type of answer required by the statement. Usually a word or phrase in the statement will provide a clue to the kind of answer you will need to supply. For example, the following statement requires that you provide the name of a baseball player:

Before Cal Ripken broke his record of consecutive major league baseball

games played, _____ _____ held that record.

answer: Lou Gehrig

Notice, too, by the way, that there are two blanks, one for the first name and another for the last name. Two blanks always indicate that two words are needed.

In the next example, it's clear that you must supply the title of a work of art.

Bernini's life-size statue, _____ , depicts the biblical hero with his

slingshot ready to hurl a stone.

answer: David

One additional tip you can use when answering fill-in questions is to look closely at the article *a* or *an* before a blank. In the first case, you will need to supply a work that begins with a consonant; in the second, a word beginning with a vowel.

Be aware, however, that some instructors will eliminate this clue by writing a question that uses *a(n)* before the blank, indicating that the word to follow could begin with either a consonant or a vowel.

Taking Essay Tests

In many of your college classes you will write essay exams. Sometimes these will be take-home tests with a specific requirement for the number of words or pages. You may be permitted to use your books or notes to answer in-class essay questions. Such "open-book" tests are usually not as easy as they may at first sound. The reason? You spend time looking through your books and notes when you could be writing. And unless you have organized your notes carefully and know where to find what you need, unless you have studied your books and materials so that you can access them quickly, you may waste precious time. One useful technique is to tab and index your text and notes so you can find your way around them quickly. Another is to color-code your notes or to use headings or symbols, either for different topics and subtopics or to indicate different degrees of importance.

Most often, your essay tests will occur in class and will prohibit any use of notes or books. What can you do to perform well on such in-class essay tests?

Let's assume that you've prepared yourself well. You've done the requisite studying. Let's also assume that you've read and understood the questions and that you are ready to get down to work. What do you do?

Essay Test-Taking Strategies

First, *budget your time.* If you have to answer three essays in an hour, you want to be sure you have time for that third question.

Second, *interpret the questions.* Be sure you understand what you are being asked to do. If the question asks for analysis, provide it. If a question asks you to "describe" or "compare" or "explain," you'll have to do precisely what it asks. Many college essay questions ask for analysis, explanation, or interpretation. That is, you will be expected not merely to parrot back information, but to explain the significance of that information. You can expect not merely to summarize the plot of a novel you've read for class, but to analyze the relationships among its characters or explain what the plot reveals about the author's ideas or attitudes.

Third, *think before you write.* Rather than simply plunging in with the first thing that occurs to you, spend a few minutes thinking about what you will say. Consider how you should approach the question efficiently and effectively. A few minutes planning and jotting a scratch outline can give your answer a logical order and clarity it might lack without such preliminary thought. Some students prepare an outline or a mind map to link areas they wish to elaborate on.

Fourth, *blend ideas with evidence,* make general points and back them up with specific examples. This is critical. Essay answers that omit specific references or concrete examples often reveal a lack of knowledge. Such answers may be superficial or vague. On the other hand, essay responses that contain only information and specific details may reveal a lack of broad understanding. You need both facts and explanations, specific details and the ideas they illustrate.

Writing strong essay exam answers is essential for success in many college courses. Answering essay examination questions poses a challenge because you are writing under the pressure of time. To write essay exam answers that demonstrate your grasp of a subject, you will have to write efficiently and effectively.

Effective preparation for an exam includes careful notetaking in class and during assigned reading. In reviewing your notes for an essay exam, look for patterns and connections among facts, examples, theories, and other forms of information. Essay exams typically require students to synthesize information gleaned from lectures and readings, to explain relationships among important events and ideas, and to evaluate them.

Here are some examples of common types of essay exam questions and the key terms you should look for in responding to them.

Key Terms to Look for in Essay Exam Questions
Identify means to name, indicate, or specify. Some essay exams include the word *identify* as part of a question that asks you to "identify and explain" or to "identify and discuss."

> Identify three prominent African-American scientists and explain their contributions to their respective fields.

Explain means to provide reasons for; to lay out causes, effects, implications, ramifications. Explanations can be simple or complex, general or specific; they can include sparse or full detail. The time limit for an essay response will determine how much or how little explanation should be provided. If you are unsure, ask for clarification.

> Explain how a legislative proposal becomes a law.

Discuss means to talk or write about. Because the instruction is not specific, it is important to know how much flexibility you have with your answer. *Discuss* is often used to mean *explain*.

> Discuss Thoreau's reasons for leaving Walden Pond.

Define means to provide a definition, to point out characteristic features, to identify limits or to put something into a category. Definitions can be brief or extended. An essay question that asks you to define a term or concept may also require that you examine, explain, elucidate, exemplify, characterize, list, or further discuss the various aspects or elements of your definition.

> Define the concept of multiculturalism. Discuss the social and political issues that the debate about multiculturalism has raised.

Compare means to consider the similarities and differences between two things.

Compare and contrast Woody Allen's movie comedies with those of Mel Brooks. Consider Allen and Brooks as both actors and directors.

Analyze means to break into parts in order to yield insight. To do an analysis of something involves examining it closely and carefully, looking at its details and at its component parts.

Analyze the structure and function of the cell.

Evaluate means to assess or make a judgment about. You may be asked to evaluate the claims made by competing theories or to evaluate the performance of a stock. Evaluation often involves comparison and explanation.

Evaluate the performance of Mel Gibson in the 1991 film *Hamlet*.

Tactics for Answering Essay Questions
Once your have read the question and understood what you are being asked to do, allow yourself a few minutes to think before you begin writing your answer. Spend some time considering what you want to say and how you might go about using what you know to support your idea. You will find that you can remember quite a bit in even a few minutes of thinking—if you are well prepared. Collect your thoughts and begin to sort them. Give some consideration as well to how much time you have to answer the question, and then allot your time sensibly. For example, if your exam includes two essay questions in a 50-minute period and if the questions are equally weighted, plan to devote equal time to each.

Begin with some preliminary writing—jotting a few rough notes in no special order. You can arrange your notes later, simply numbering them as you prepare to write your full essay response. The very act of putting pen on paper should stimulate further thought and help you make connections among all that you have studied and learned. You can also order your notes in a scratch outline, noting how you can begin and end your essay and identifying some points to cover in between. By making a rough sketch of where you are heading and how you plan to get there, you will decrease the chances of forgetting something important. You will also enhance the organization and readability of your answer. Try, even in your rough preliminary notes, to include a thesis statement that responds concretely and specifically to the question.

Reviewing Your Answer
As you write, be sure to respond directly to the question. Avoid vagueness and bland generalizations. Also avoid trying to throw everything you can think of into your answer; instead, tackle the question head-on. Avoiding a direct response to the question will deprive your answer of clarity and focus and will diminish the point you wish to make.

For example, consider the following question:

Discuss the economic factors that led up to the Civil War.

This very specific question requires an answer that addresses economic factors only—not political, military, or religious ones. (Unless, of course, you can show how those other kinds of factors directly relate to the economic issues the question calls for.) You also do not want to answer a broad question too narrowly. Respond to a question that asks how divorce affects children in the United States by providing information, statistics, evidence, and arguments specifically about all kinds of effects of divorce on children (social and psychological effects as well as financial and other effects). You should not stray from the question, however, by discussing the causes of divorce or its effects on divorcing couples.

The most important thing you can do when writing an essay exam is to attend carefully to what the question asks for and then to be specific and thorough in providing an answer that demonstrates what you know. You will also want to write quickly. Although you may be more comfortable with slow, leisurely writing, in a timed test you simply do not have that luxury. Rapid writing may also help stimulate additional thinking. As you write out one detail or example, you may think of another. And, finally, be sure to reserve a few minutes to review your answer. If you do not have this time, so be it. But try to build in even a few minutes for reviewing your writing. As you review, you may discover that you overlooked a telling detail, an important issue, or a significant fact. Or you may find that you left out a word or phrase that would make your sentence more intelligible. You may even find that you wrote the opposite of what you intended. Moreover, you can clean up surface writing errors, such as misspelled words or misused or confusing punctuation.

When you find yourself running short of time in an essay exam, map out the direction your essay would take if you had time to complete it. Provide an outline for the instructor, showing him or her what you intended to discuss. Depending on how specific you can make the outline and on how accurate and thorough you have been up to that point, you should receive a better grade than you would if you simply stopped in midstream.

Avoiding Cheating

With the pressures to succeed in college, you may observe students cheating. You yourself may be tempted to cheat. In any and all cases, do not. If you're unprepared for a surprise quiz, suffer the consequences and be better prepared next time. If you're tempted to copy answers from other students on big tests, or if you're inclined to buy a term paper rather than write your own, you need to consider why. And you need to consider the consequences of your actions—whether or not you get caught.

Besides being a form of theft, cheating undermines the integrity of academic institutions. To participate in the work of an academic community requires abiding by its rules and accepting its conventions. Cheating violates those conventions.

One type of cheating, *plagiarism,* involves appropriating the ideas of another and pretending they are yours. When you use someone else's ideas or words, whether you use them in a paper or in a speech, you must credit your source. Not to do so, claiming authorship of words or ideas you did not develop on your own, is dishonest. Nearly all colleges and universities take plagiarism seriously; some, in fact, dismiss students for plagiarizing.

Be sure you understand the different forms plagiarism can take. And be sure you understand different instructors' definitions of the term. Consult a good college handbook, and talk about plagiarism with your advisor or with one of your instructors.

Exercise 7-6

According to your college bulletin, what penalties are exacted for plagiarism. Consult a college handbook, a university statement, or a guide to research that illustrates plagiarism in its various forms and degrees of severity.

Chapter 8

Reading with Understanding

Chapter Highlights

This chapter is based on the assumption that reading is an important key to educational success. Reading is important not merely for acquiring information but also in developing your thinking, especially your ability to analyze and interpret. Reading also develops your vocabulary. Beyond these practical values, reading also offers considerable pleasures. In encouraging and prompting better reading habits, this chapter includes the following topics:

- Myths about reading
- Reasons for reading
- Reading for information
- Reading and interpretation
- Reading and evaluation
- Reading and imagination
- Reading as conversation
- Reading strategies
- Forms of Analysis

Key Questions

Here are a few questions to consider as you begin this chapter:

1. Why are you reading this chapter, these words, this book?

2. What do you read on your own, for pleasure?
3. Has reading been more a pleasure or a duty for you? Why?
4. What do you do when you read something you don't understand at first?
5. Why do you read or do you not read?

Myths about Reading

Sometimes popular ideas can interfere with our ability to learn. You may have heard, for example, that if you don't learn a foreign language early, you can never learn one. Or you may be familiar with the idea that females have trouble learning math and science—that males are somehow innately better at learning these subjects. Similar myths exist about reading. Here are a few of the more common ones, followed by a response that offers an alternative perspective.

Myth 1

Reading isn't really necessary in today's world of rapidly developing technology. Movies and television, cameras and computers, telephones and telecommunication have made reading obsolete.

Response: If computers are making reading obsolete, then why are so many books, manuals, and magazines about computing being published? To take full advantage of the technology that continues to be developed and refined, reading is necessary for understanding how that technology works. The speed with which technological developments occur, in fact, results in voluminous information that needs to be processed.

The importance of reading is also a given for visual media such as television and the movie industry, in which scripts must be read and learned before they can be performed, whether the performer is an actor in a movie or an anchor on the television evening news. You might also argue, further, that computers provide simply another environment for reading—E-mail, for example.

Myth 2

Speed reading is better than slow reading; faster is somehow better.

Response: There is no question that reading fast has its uses. You use speed reading to skim news articles, to survey a chapter in a textbook, to get a quick overview of a writer's basic idea and approach. But speed reading has its limits. And it does not suit all reading occasions and purposes. Though it is useful for acquiring information, speed reading is not very useful for promoting thinking. To complement fast reading, you need to learn a slower, more reflective type of reading in which you deliberate or weigh and consider what you are reading. You need to read slowly, carefully, and thoughtfully whenever you encounter new material and whenever what you read requires reflection, even when the material is relatively familiar.

Myth 3

Written works should never be challenged or questioned.

Response: This is not only patently false, it is also dangerous. It is certainly true that some texts are believed to contain revealed truth—the Bible and the Koran, for example. But not even all those who believe in these texts refuse to question or challenge them.

Related to this myth is the idea that if something appears in print it must be true and thus worthy of our assent. That a statement or an idea appears in print, however, is no guarantee that it is correct or intelligent. Newspapers, for example, are notorious for getting the facts of a story wrong—sometimes significant facts seriously wrong. What's true of newspapers can also apply to books, pamphlets, and other publications. Just because something appears in print in a book does not mean it is worthy of belief.

Myth 4

Reading is a passive experience, one that is more virtual than real. Readers aren't really doing anything when they read.

Response: Reading is no less active than writing or speaking, mowing the lawn, or doing the week's shopping. It is a mental and intellectual rather than a physical activity; what gets produced is thought. Reading is connected with the real world since reality is as much internal (in our minds) as external. Spending time reading is as valuable as time spent doing many other things we do. The reason? Because our intellectual and imaginative powers are called more fully into play when we read. Think, for example, of how many times the movie version of a book is less interesting than the original book itself.

Taking Stock

Can you identify any other myths about reading? What are some of your own thoughts about reading? What kinds of reading do you do? Why?

Exercise 8-1

Interview three people about their reading habits and their thoughts about reading: a friend who reads, a family member, and a teacher. Identify any common elements you discover in their reading experiences.

Reasons for Reading

Reading is essential for the kinds of learning college requires. Heavy reading is expected of college students, reading that will also challenge you with its level of difficulty. The better you can read—the better you can understand and analyze what you read—the better you will learn.

We read for different reasons: to escape, to pass time, to acquire information, to understand, to think, to learn, to experience, to enjoy ourselves. Our purposes differ, and so, too, do the ways we read. Sometimes we read less to understand than simply to acquire information, to collect facts and figures. Sometimes we read to understand writers' ideas or to share their experience. We may read to think through an issue or problem, to weigh and consider, to evaluate the merits of an argument, to make judgments and to better understand why we make the judgments we do.

To improve your reading, try to increase your reading repertoire by developing an ability to read in the following ways:

Reading actively: reading with a pen in hand, underlining, annotating, jotting notes in a book's margins and inside covers
Reading reflectively: reading slowly and deliberately; considering and weighing what you read and challenging it when necessary
Reading interpretively: reading to understand; making sense of what a writer is saying; coming to a sense of its central idea
Reading evaluatively: reading to evaluate the persuasiveness of what you read; assessing not only the quality of the content but also the values and ideals it reflects

Reading for Information

One of the most common reasons for reading is to acquire information. In the simplest form of reading-for-information, your goal may be to gather facts. You may want to know how to operate your new VCR or how much it costs to travel from Chicago to San Francisco. You may want to know what happened in the United States during the first week of July in 1863. You may want to collect information about wolves or whales. Or you may simply read a book or magazine out of curiosity or interest. Along the way you will almost certainly pick up information.

The following excerpt from an essay published in a popular magazine provides information about trees. Read it to see what you can learn.

Street Trees

David Quammen

According to Adrian Benepe, there are more than 600,000 street trees (and another two million park trees) in New York City. Each year the Department of Transportation plants about 10,000 trees, replacing other trees that have been injured or removed in the course of road construction. Mr. Benepe's own department, Parks and Recreation, plants another 10,000 trees. No tree is cut down unless it is dead, terminally ill and potentially infectious, or in the path of the Transportation Department, and yet those 20,000 annual plantings are barely enough to keep up with attrition. Some sources even say that attrition is running ahead of the replanting, and that New York is moving slowly, sadly, toward treelessness.

What drives the attrition? Most of New York's street trees suffer from too little water and too much heat. During respiration (yes, trees do breathe) they absorb sulfur dioxide, hydrogen cyanide, hydrogen fluoride, peroxyacetyl nitrates, ethylene, and other noxious gases that can inhibit photosynthesis, disrupt their enzyme activity, and damage their foliage. City dust also tends to clog leaf pores, which further reduces photosynthesis and respiration and can literally cause a tree to suffocate. Weakened by such forms of stress, a city tree is all the more vulnerable to parasitic insects or some microbial malady like anthracnose, Dutch elm disease, canker, oak wilt. Even these problems, according to Benepe, are not the worst of it. "I once saw a tree that died quickly after an exterminator poured his exterminating liquid on its roots." And then again there's the poisonous insult of dog urine, contributed to the environment of New York's streets at the rate of roughly 22,000 gallons a day. Small wonder that the life expectancy of a tree in Manhattan is only seven years. It's not easy being green in that place.

In reading this kind of passage, you acquire information—figures, such as the number of trees in New York City, and facts, such as New York's gradually decreasing tree population. More important than absorbing these facts and figures, however, is the need to relate such information to the writer's idea or point. In this case the point is explicit and clear: New York City's trees are in danger from a wide range of contaminants, from noxious gases to exterminating fluids to dog urine. These poisons, coupled with insufficient light, water, and excessive heat, reduce the life expectancy of a typical tree to a mere seven years. That last fact is shocking both in itself and because it is a consequence of the other facts that Quammen marshals.

Thus, even though your primary aim in reading such a piece may be to find things out, you may also discover yourself thinking about the information you glean. Most of your college reading requires not merely that you obtain facts but that you understand the writer's point and then relate that point to what you already know. You can use the following questions as guidelines:

1. What is the subject of the piece?
2. What is being said about that subject?
3. To what extent can you relate the piece to what you know?
4. What connections can you make among the details of the piece?
5. What do those details and connections add up to?

Exercise 8-2

Read an article from a news magazine and use the preceding questions to help you arrive at the writer's point.

Exercise 8-3

Apply the reading-for-information questions to a chapter from one of your textbooks.

Reading and Interpretation

To *interpret* is to make sense of something. You do this regularly in your everyday life. You make sense of what people say to you. You interpret gestures such as a traffic officer's holding up an open palm; you interpret the various looks people give you, reading their facial expressions and body movements. You interpret actions to make sense of what people do as well as what they say. You cannot avoid interpreting. Nor should you, for interpretation is basic to everyday living. It is also essential for academic success.

Here is a short piece of writing for you to interpret.

Learning to Be Silent

The pupils of the Tendai school used to study meditation before Zen entered Japan. Four of them who were intimate friends promised one another to observe seven days of silence.

On the first day all were silent. Their meditation had begun auspiciously, but when night came and the oil lamps were growing dim one of the pupils could not help exclaiming to a servant: "Fix those lamps."

The second pupil was surprised to hear the first one talk. "We are not supposed to say a word," he remarked.

"You two are stupid. Why did you talk?" asked the third.

"I am the only one who has not talked," concluded the fourth pupil.

How do you go about understanding this text? First, consider its subject—silence. Ask yourself what the piece seems to show or suggest about this subject. To do that, consider its details. Essentially, there is one kind of detail—the comment each friend makes. To understand the story, we must relate the friends' comments to one another and to the overall meaning of the story. Since this idea is implied rather than stated outright, we need to make inferences about it.

Making Inferences

An *inference* is a statement we make about what we don't know based on what we do know. To infer is to think, to make a mental leap from information or details to an idea about that information or those details.

Your inferences will lead you to an understanding of what you are reading. In the case of "Learning to Be Silent," it helps to know that the story is a *parable*, a story with an implied moral or lesson. Perhaps you have read parables before. If you have never read a parable, you almost certainly have read fables—animal stories with morals about human behavior. In any event it is our task as readers to infer the lesson the parable teaches.

We might formulate the point of the parable like this: "Learning to be silent is more difficult than it appears to be." Or: "Silence is nearly impossible to maintain." Or: "Competition breeds contempt; cooperation is more effective." Or: (supply your own moral). The parable's moral or point can be stated in a variety of ways. Different readers will understand that point differently. They will interpret the story in different ways, which is both inescapable and desirable.

This does not mean, however, that you can simply say anything you like about the text. The meanings you derive from it should be available for others

---

Taking Stock

Before reading on, take stock of your experience in reading stories like this one. Try to connect at least one aspect of the story to your previous experience (a religious aspect, an educational context, or a humorous incident, for example).

---

to see and understand as well. Although we may see different things in a text, we also see some of the same things. And although we need not all understand a text in exactly the same way, it is useful to have our more farfetched notions reined in by the understanding of other readers. Through the eyes of other readers, in fact, we often discover meanings we miss by ourselves.

Exercise 8-4

Write out two morals that capture the meaning of "Learning to be Silent." Write each as a single, separate sentence.

Moral 1 _____

Moral 2 _____

Reading and Evaluation

In describing reading to interpret, we emphasized the necessity of submitting to the text. When you submit to the text, you give the author a chance to make his or her point without prematurely judging its merit or value. When you read interpretively, the writer's meaning is primary.

In reading to *evaluate*, however, you may find yourself resisting the claims of the text. You may decide, for example, that a text's ideas are unconvincing or that you don't endorse its values. You submit to a text to understand it, but you often resist a text when evaluating it.

In reading to evaluate, your goal is different from understanding. Although you must understand a writer's point to make a fair and reasoned judgment about it, your goal in evaluative reading is to make a judgment, to consider the merits of the text.

The following questions can help you read evaluatively.

1. Have you ever heard this idea before? Where and in what context(s)?
2. Is the idea convincing? Why or why not?

3. Is the idea appealing? Do you like it? Why or why not?
4. Does this idea lead you anywhere? To another idea, perhaps? To additional kinds of support for it?
5. Does your own experience confirm the idea or cause you to question it?

In raising such questions and in tentatively answering them, you should give the writer's idea a fair chance. Try to consider the reader's idea thoughtfully and carefully rather than simply rejecting it outright. Be aware also that your assessment of any idea can change. An idea that you find outlandish today might seem more than reasonable in the future. And conversely, an idea you find convincing and interesting now may seem silly a few months or a few years from now.

An additional point: When we evaluate a writer's idea, we think about it attentively. We weigh it, seeking its strengths and weaknesses, its possibilities and its limits. We deliberate about it, slowing down our thinking process sufficiently to consider it thoughtfully. This kind of reflective thinking is illustrated in the following comments about "Learning to Be Silent."

On "Learning to Be Silent"

We may wonder why the young monks are practicing silence and what value it holds for them. In some religious traditions such as Buddhism, asceticism is highly valued. One aspect of the ascetic ideal involves self-denial, self-discipline, self-control. Thus silence has value because it centers the mind and spirit on what are considered essential spiritual realities. Since so much talk concerns trivial matters, one way to avoid distractions is to practice silence.

If, on the other hand, you do not see much value in keeping silent, either to collect your thoughts or to discipline your spirit, you might make a very different evaluation of the ideal held out in the parable. In fact, you might even say that it was better for the monks to break their silence. You might argue that their talk held advantages that outweighed their keeping quiet.

Reading and Imagination

To read is to imagine. When we read, we imagine a voice in our heads, perhaps a person or *persona*—a figure or character behind the voice. That's the first way in which our minds activate our imagination in reading. But there's much more to our imaginative response.

Reading stimulates our imagination, calling it into active life. In awakening our imagination, reading exercises and enlightens it. What does it mean to *imagine*? And what is involved in the act of *imagining*? What, in short, is *imagination*?

All three forms of the word have two important things in common. First, all refer to the play of mind, to the active power of creative thinking. Second, the heart of all these words is *image*. Usually we speak or think of an image as something we can visualize or see in our mind's eye. For some reading, this kind of mental seeing is particularly important. But the imaginative response is not confined to this kind of mental seeing. Some texts will evoke other imaginative responses, serving to stimulate our senses of touch, taste, smell, or hearing.

Using Your Imagination

Let your imagination go to work on the following passage, a description of a place and a person and the world associated with them.

> A single knoll rises out of the plain in Oklahoma, north and west of the Wichita range. For my people, the Kiowas, it is an old landmark, and they gave it the name Rainy Mountain. The hardest weather in the world is there. Winter brings blizzards, hot tornadic winds arise in the spring, and in summer the prairie is an anvil's edge. The grass turns brittle and brown, and it cracks beneath your feet. There are green belts along the rivers and creeks, linear groves of hickory and pecan, willow and witch hazel. At a distance in July or August the streaming foliage seems almost to writhe in fire. Great green and yellow grasshoppers are everywhere in the tall grass, popping up like corn to sting the flesh, and tortoises crawl about on the red earth, going nowhere in the plenty of time. Loneliness is an aspect of the land. All things in the plain are isolate; there is no confusion of objects in the eye, but one hill or one tree or one man. To look upon that landscape in the early morning, with the sun at your back, is to lose the sense of proportion. Your imagination comes to life, and this, you think, is where Creation was begun. . . .
>
> Now that I can have her only in memory, I see my grandmother in the several postures that were peculiar to her: standing at the wood stove on a winter morning and turning meat in a great iron skillet; sitting at the south window, bent above her beadwork, and afterwards, when her vision failed, looking down for a long time into the fold of her hands; going out upon a cane, very slowly as she did when the weight of age came upon her; praying. I remember her most often at prayer. She made long, rambling prayers out of suffering and hope, having seen many things. I was never sure that I had the right to hear, so exclusive were they of all mere custom and company. The last time I saw her she prayed standing by the side of her bed at night, naked to the waist, the light of a kerosene lamp moving upon her dark skin. Her long black hair, always drawn and braided in the day, lay upon her shoulders and

against her breasts like a shawl. I do not speak Kiowa, and I never understood her prayers, but there was something inherently sad in the sound, some merest hesitation upon the syllables of sorrow. She began in a high and descending pitch, exhausting her breath to silence; then again and again—and always the same intensity of effort, of something that is, and is not, like urgency in the human voice. Transported so in the dancing light among the shadows of her room, she seemed beyond the reach of time. But that was illusion; I think I knew then that I should not see her gain.

Source: N. Scott Momaday, *The Way to Rainy Mountain*

Momaday invites us to imagine a particular person and place. His carefully selected language and detail help us to imagine what he describes. We see with him the brown and green grass. We feel the hard ground and hear the dry brittle grass crack. We sense how the grandeur of this landscape stimulates Momaday's memory and imagination all the while he is stimulating ours. In his recollection of his grandmother, Momaday conveys an impression of beauty, simplicity, and grandeur. In evoking his grandmother for himself in imagination, he shares with us his reverent image of her.

The Power of Imagination

Your imaginative faculty does more than just stimulate your senses. Imagination also leads you to think, shift perspectives, understand another's point of view. Imagination enables you to feel another's pain, share his or her joy. Imagination allows you to extend the boundaries of your life, helping you to a more richly textured and a more widely varied set of experiences.

Consider your imagination as a talent that ought to be developed, a muscle that requires strengthening, a habit that deserves cultivation. Your imagination is too rich a resource, too precious a commodity to lie buried, underdeveloped, and undervalued.

Try to take advantage of opportunities to use your imagination frequently in class and out. The chapters of this book invite you to use your imagination through Taking Stock invitations and the exercises. Chapter 12 on creative thinking also provides guidance and practice in using your imagination.

Exercise 8-5

Read an advertisement, story, poem, essay, or article that you consider especially imaginative. Bring it to class for discussion. Why is it imaginative? What images, visual and literal, make an impact on you? Why?

Reading as Conversation

One way to experience what reading involves is to approach it as an interaction with the author. Imagine yourself in dialogue not simply with a text but with a person, with a writer whose voice you hear and whose mind you come to know.

It takes two to converse—to dialogue. Imagining the writer behind the text and envisioning how the writer might respond to your queries and reactions to the text provides an additional way into a work. It can lead you to discover different things than you might see with other approaches.

Exercise 8-6

Take the imaginative reading you did for the N. Scott Momaday passage and write six questions you would like to ask the writer. Choose three of them and try to imagine how the writer might respond to them.

Question 1 _____

Question 2 _____

Question 3 _____

Question 4 _____

Question 5 _____

Question 6 _____

Response 1 _____

_____

Response 2 _____

_____

Response 3 _____

_____

Reading and Personal Response

Reacting to a Text

Our preliminary response to any experience is what we might call simply a gut reaction. We react to things instinctively, sometimes emotionally, and always subjectively. And we react to written texts the same way we react to people that we meet and experiences that we undergo. Initially, of course, your responses to a writer's thought will not be fully formed since they will be tied up with making sense of what you are reading. But as you read, your impressions of the text and your intellectual and emotional responses to it will solidify and intensify.

One way to begin making note of your reactions to what you read is to jot annotations in the margins. These can record your feelings as well as your thoughts about the text.

Here is a brief text that has been underlined and annotated.

Is beauty really essential? Seems exaggerated.

To be called beautiful is thought to name something essential to women's character and concerns. (In contrast to men—whose essence is to be strong, or effective, or competent.) It does not take someone in the throes of

Society defines norms of beauty. Women are pushed into overconcern with their appearance.

advanced feminist awareness to perceive that the way women are taught to be involved with beauty encourages narcissism, reinforces dependence and immaturity. Everybody (women and men) knows that. For it is "everybody," a whole society, that has identified being feminine with caring about how one *looks*. (In contrast to being masculine—

Contrast: men do well; women look good.

which is identified with caring about what one *is* and *does* and only secondarily, if at all, about how one looks.) Given these stereotypes, it is no wonder that beauty enjoys, at best, a rather mixed reputation.

Contrast: desire for beauty vs. obligation to be beautiful.

It is not, of course, the desire to be beautiful that is wrong but the obligation to be—or to try. What is accepted by most women as a flattering idealization of their sex is a way of making women feel inferior to what they actually

S. politicizes the issue—beauty as a means of oppression.

are—or normally grow to be. For the ideal of beauty is administered as a form of self-oppression. Women are taught to see their bodies in *parts*, and to evaluate each part

Women + beauty = body parts.

separately. Breasts, feet, hips, waistline, neck, eyes, nose, complexion, hair, and so on—each in turn is submitted to an anxious, fretful, often despairing scrutiny. Even if some pass muster, some will always be found wanting. Nothing less than perfection will do.

Doesn't S. exaggerate here about perfection?

In men, good looks is a whole, something taken in at a glance. It does not need to be confirmed by giving measurements of different regions of the body; nobody

Nice distinction here on beauty and the sexes.

encourages a man to dissect his appearance, feature by feature. As for perfection, that is considered trivial—almost unmanly. Indeed, in the ideally good-looking man a small

!!! Imperfections acceptable in men. Hmm . . . Redford's mole?

imperfection or blemish is considered positively desirable.

Source: Susan Sontag, "A Woman's Beauty: Put-Down or Power Source?"

Exercise 8-7

Jot down a few extra annotations to the passage.

Reflecting

Your preliminary impressions of the text will often lead you to further thoughts about it. If you are sufficiently engaged or affected by the writing, you will begin to think along with the writer. On one hand, you begin to follow his or her line of thought. On the other, you begin to think about what is being said. (We are still talking of first thoughts, of preliminary acts of mind—not thorough understanding by means of considered, full-scale analysis.)

One way to reflect on a text in this preliminary way is to do some *focused freewriting.* Jot down your response to a text without worrying about the logical ordering of your thoughts, simply putting down what occurs to you in the order it occurs. Because freewriting is more sustained than annotation, it provides a way to pursue an idea, to develop your thinking to see where it may lead. Freewriting can help you discover what interests you in a text. Although, like annotation, it is preliminary to sustained thoughtful analysis and interpretation, free writing is nevertheless one way to reflect on your reading.

Here is an example of freewriting reflections based on the previously annotated passage.

Example of Freewriting

Interesting questions. Women do seem to think more about their looks than men do. But since it's men women wish to please by looking good, men may be responsible (some? much?) for women's obsession with appearance. How far have women bought into the beauty myth? How far are they responsible for obsessing about beauty? How about money and profit? And at whose expense?

Why don't men *need* to be beautiful? To please parents—employers? To attract a mate? To be considered "normal"? Sontag says that beauty is irrelevant to men—men judged by different measures—strength, effectiveness, competence. She doesn't mention power, money, status. She leaves things out—intelligence and moral qualities—kindness, decency, generosity. How important are these? For women?

Distinction between *desiring* to be beautiful (perhaps to be desired or admired) and *needing* to be. There's nothing wrong with women wanting to be attractive, to look their best. The problem occurs when desire becomes *obligation*, wasting women's talents, minimizes them, keeps them subservient.

Parts and wholes—are women concerned with *parts* of their bodies—certain parts? Their overall appearance? Their sense of self? Silicone breast implants? Cosmetic surgery generally? (But: men have nose jobs, facelifts, even pectoral implants.) Men are concerned with some parts of their bodies more than with others—though for different reasons?

What about the words used to describe good-looking women—or good-looking men? A "beautiful" woman but a "handsome" man. A "foxy" lady, a "gorgeous" woman (guy?), an "attractive" girl, a ??? And what of men? "Handsome" does most of the work. So too does "good-looking." Though we also have "pretty boy" and "hunk"—derogatory (and dated?). Hmm. Statuesque? Powerfully built? A real he-man.? A!??

Exercise 8-8

Add a few of your own reflections about the passage.

Considering

Another way to reflect on a text is to do a *stop-and-go reading* of it. With this technique you simply read part of the text (a few sentences or paragraphs, depending on the length of the work) and then begin writing. After jotting some observations, thoughts, and questions, pick up where you left off reading and continue until another stopping point, where you again should pause and write.

In a stop-and-go reading, you read with an increasingly sharper alertness to the text since you are thinking about it carefully while you read. The procedure forces you to slow down. In the process, you notice things you would normally overlook. Sometimes you can actually watch your ideas emerge as you look back at portions of the text you have read and anticipate what is to come.

Here is an example of the technique used with the first two paragraphs of an essay about men. The author, Gretel Ehrlich, originally published her essay in *Time* magazine.

> When I'm in New York but feeling lonely for Wyoming I look for the Marlboro ads in the subway. What I'm aching to see is horseflesh, the glint of a spur, a line of distant mountains, brimming creeks, and a reminder of the ranchers and cowboys I've ridden with for the last eight years. But the men I see in

those posters with their stern, humorless looks remind me of no one I know there. In our hellbent earnestness to romanticize the cowboy we've ironically disesteemed his true character. If he's "strong and silent" it's because there's probably no one to talk to. If he "rides away into the sunset" it's because he's been on horseback since four in the morning moving cattle and he's trying, fifteen hours later, to get home to his family. If he's "a rugged individualist" he's also part of a team: ranch work is teamwork and even the glorified open-range cowboys of the 1880s rode up and down the Chisholm Trail in the company of twenty or thirty other riders. Instead of the macho, trigger-happy man our culture has perversely wanted him to be, the cowboy is more apt to be convivial, quirky, and softhearted. To be "tough" on a ranch has nothing to do with conquests and displays of power. More often than not, circumstances—like the colt he's riding or an unexpected blizzard—are overpowering him. It's not toughness but "toughing it out" that counts. In other words, this macho, cultural artifact the cowboy has become is simply a man who possesses resilience, patience, and an instinct for survival. "Cowboys are just like a pile of rocks—everything happens to them. They get climbed on, kicked, rained and snowed on, scuffed up by wind. Their job is "just to take it," one old-timer told me.

Ehrlich corrects what she considers an inaccurate stereotype of the cowboy. She begins with a reference to this stereotype (the Marlboro cowboy) and offers a more complex understanding of the image created by the ad. She works from the stereotype to show how the conventional image and idea are inadequate, how they oversimplify and misrepresent reality. In contrasting the conventional understanding of a cowboy's character with her own perspective, Ehrlich uses cowboy speech to help characterize them.

A cowboy is someone who loves his work. Since the hours are long—ten to fifteen hours a day—and the pay is $30 he has to. What's required of him is an odd mixture of physical vigor and maternalism. His part of the beef-raising industry is to birth and nurture calves and take care of their mothers. For the most part his work is done on horseback and in a lifetime he sees and comes to know more animals than people. The iconic myth surrounding him is built on American notions of heroism: the index of a man's value as measured in physical courage. Such ideas have perverted manliness into a self-absorbed race for cheap thrills. In a rancher's world, courage has less to do with facing danger than with acting spontaneously—usually on behalf of an animal or another rider. If a cow is stuck in the boghole he throws a loop around her neck, takes his daily (a half hitch around the saddle horn), and pulls her out with horsepower. If a calf is born sick, he may take her home, warm her in front of the kitchen fire, and massage her legs until dawn. One friend, whose favorite horse was trying to swim a lake with hobbles on, dove under water and cut her legs loose with a knife, then swam her to shore, his arms around her neck lifeguard-style, and saved her from drowning. Because these incidents are usually linked to someone or something outside himself, the westerner's courage is selfless, a form of compassion.

Ehrlich's second paragraph, which continues to play off the stereotype she began with, increases our understanding of what a cowboy's life is really like. Here she talks about "courage" and "heroism"—popular virtues associated with the cowboy. Instead of denying the importance of these virtues for cowboys, Ehrlich reinterprets them, explaining that cowboys act courageously, not out of some macho need to prove themselves in the face of danger, but out of necessity, often on behalf of another cowboy or on behalf of an animal. A key word for her in this respect is *compassion*, one of Ehrlich's apparent requirements for successful cowboy life. And for Ehrlich compassion is linked with *maternalism*, which she associates with the cowboy's selflessness.

Forms of Analysis

Complementing your subjective response to what you read is a more objective approach to analysis and interpretation. Along with your preliminary impressions of a text, your liking and disliking, approving and disapproving, you should also try to understand what the author's words mean. And even though it may be difficult to eliminate your subjective reactions and to prevent yourself from remaking the author's text in your image, you must try to understand the author's perspective, not merely to formulate your own. You need to see the otherness of the writer's text and not merely your own reflection in it as in a mirror.

From Observation to Interpretation

You can do the more objective and analytical kind of reading by following four steps: observing, connecting, inferring, and concluding. Let's take them one at a time.

Observing

Perhaps the most important step toward interpretation is the first—making observations. Since you can't say more than you can see, it is essential to look and notice, to discern and perceive what a text contains. Your interpretation of a text is only as good as the evidence that supports it. And that evidence, essentially, is what you notice, the observations you can make about the text.

An *observation*, in fact, can be described simply as the result of an act of noticing. You may notice, for example, that a text is written in short or long paragraphs or that its sentences vary in length or form. You may see that particular words or images recur, or that the writer uses many contractions or few, that he or she uses comparisons profusely or sparingly. Perhaps you will notice something about the overall structure of the text—that it begins and ends in a similar way; that it makes a point implicitly rather than explicitly; that it tells a story or a series of stories, perhaps in chronological order, perhaps not; that it compares or contrasts or classifies ideas or facts; that its tone is formal or informal, its style direct and straightforward or more oblique and complex. There is literally no end to the number and kind of observations we can make about texts.

Such acts of attention, however, are not enough. They are only the beginning. From them we begin to notice other things, patterns most importantly— patterns of contrast, of repetition, of emphasis. We discern a relationship among the things we notice. And thus while we are still engaged in "noticing," we are doing that noticing at a higher intellectual level, the level of making connections and discovering relationships.

Exercise 8-9

Make a list of observations about Ehrlich's passage or Sontag's (see pp. 131, 133–135). Or choose a passage from an assigned reading for one of your courses.

Connecting

To make a connection is to see one thing in relation to another. To establish or discover a relationship between two things is, essentially, to begin thinking. Thinking involves putting things together, seeing how they fit, and what you might make of that. Making observations and connections will engage you in mindful activity essential for successful academic work.

One value in making connections among textual details is that you forestall jumping prematurely to a conclusion. Another advantage is that you can make more than one kind of connection (that you can perceive the text's different implications). This is important because even though you will eventually arrive at one interpretation of the text, you need to acknowledge that no interpretation is absolute or definitive.

When you notice particular features of a text and begin to discern relationships among those observed details, you don't do so in discrete and separately compartmentalized ways. That is, instead of saying to yourself, "Now I am making observations and not making connections," you will surely find yourself doing both things simultaneously. In fact, one of the more important consequences of observing and connecting is that you begin noticing details previously overlooked. Moreover, you add the newly noticed details to ones previously noticed, enriching and complicating your sense of the text's implications. Finally, as you encounter still other details, you may find that some of them do not fit in with the patterns and connections you had been forming as you read. When this happens, you can do a number of things. One is simply to ignore the details that don't fit. (This, of course, is usually not a good idea, since those details have been included for a reason.)

Another option is to reconsider the connections and relationships you have established up to that point to see if there isn't some other different or larger frame of reference that will permit the inclusion of the seemingly incongruous details. Whichever option you pursue, you should also remain aware that still other details may affect your sense of how the text's details are related to convey meaning.

Exercise 8-10

Make some connections among your observations for Exercise 8-9.

Inferring

Once you have observed details and made some connections, you need to ask yourself an important question: What do these textual observations and relationships suggest, what do they imply? To answer, you must make a leap of inference. An *inference* is a guess about meaning based on your observations, a statement about the unknown (your interpretation) made on the basis of the known (what you have observed). There is no escaping the making of inferences. Without inferences you remain in the realm of observation, short of your goal of interpretation, of a reasoned understanding of a text.

You can make inferences well or you can make them poorly. Your inferences can be right or wrong, correct or incorrect. You make inferences in everyday life all the time, and thus there is nothing mysterious about the process of making them when you read. If you see someone at 8 A.M. in a classroom building with a large ring of keys opening a classroom door, you may infer that he or she is a member of the school staff, whose job it is to unlock classroom doors. You may, of course, be right or wrong about your inference, but you will have made an inference nonetheless. You may infer that students who say they don't care about grades and then proceed to study assiduously are either lying or deceiving themselves. Again, you make an interpretive guess about them based on what you see them do and relating it to what you hear them say.

But let's consider a textual example of inference making.

Here is a short text:

The old dog barks backward without getting up.
I can remember when he was a pup.

If you think this is a poem, you have made an inference, a reasonably assured one since you can point to details about the text that support that inference. But it is an inference nonetheless. Suppose we were to agree that this text is indeed a poem—on the basis of its rhyme, its similar number of syllables per line, and its contrast between the old and young dog. In that case we would be making an argument, building a case in support of our inference. But we would have to remain open to the possibility that someone might see these lines as representing another type of discourse, perhaps imagining them as appearing as an epitaph on a dog's tombstone. Never mind that you may find this unconvincing. Simply allow for the prospect of someone's suggesting it, making that inference about similar details, perhaps the very same details used to arrive at our "This is a poem" inference.

But let's go further and make another inference about this text, about this poem, if we agree to call it that.

Inference 2: This poem is not about dogs at all; it's about people.

Why is this an inference? Because the poem does not say anything particular about people. (In fact, the only word referring to a person is "I.")

Where does this inference come from? Can it be justified?

Asking such questions requires that you do a number of things if you are to consider them seriously and work toward answering them. First, they send you back to the text for a closer look. They invite you to see what else you might notice that you didn't notice before. Second, they invite you to consider an idea that may not have occurred to you before. At this point you may ask yourself whether the inference is possibly true rather than verifiable. (Remember that observations about texts should be verifiable—that is, capable of being checked and shown as true or false.) Inferences are not verifiable in the same way that observations are because inferences make an interpretive leap beyond the facts, beyond the verifiable details and into the realm of idea. Inferences are speculative. They involve thought. They lead you to consider meanings. That is both their virtue and their value.

Instead of proving to your audience than an inference is correct, you try to persuade them that it is reliable. The evidence you use to do so includes the observations you make about the text. But it must also extend beyond them. Your evidence may refer to other information you have about the text. (In our case, the fact that the author of the couplet, or pair of rhymed lines, is Robert Frost.) It may involve your knowledge of other texts similar to or different from this one. (In this case, you could argue that the couplet is a common poetic form—in fact, one of the most common and popular of short poetic forms in literature.) And you could try to find this work among Frost's poems even without its title, which you would eventually discover: "The Span of Life." And on the basis of this title, you could infer once again that the poem is about a life span—about growing old—which encompasses but is not restricted to the lives of dogs.

The important thing is that you must not be afraid to make inferences. Don't let a fear of being wrong stand in your way. To interpret and analyze texts (and data of all kinds) you must be willing to take a chance, to let go and leap to making inferences.

Exercise 8-11

Select a brief text from the reading for one of your courses and make three inferences based on observations you make about it. If you wish, you can base your inferences on the observations you listed for Exercise 8-9 or the connections you established in Exercise 8-10.

Exercise 8-12

This is the first sentence of Tolstoy's novel *Anna Karenina:* "All happy families resemble one another; all unhappy families differ, each suffering unhappiness in its own way." What inferences can you make about the novel based on this sentence?

Make two inferences based on the opening sentence of Jane Austen's *Pride and Prejudice:* "It is a truth universally acknowledged that a single man in possession of a good fortune must be in want of a wife."

What further inferences might you make about nineteenth-century novels based on your reading of these two novels' opening sentences?

Concluding

You can think of interpreting a text as a way of collecting and connecting the inferences you make about it. In the same way that you make connections among your observations, you make connections among your inferences.

Taking Stock

How often do you make inferences in the readings for your courses? Have you been hesitant about making them because of a fear about being wrong or sounding stupid? If so, what would you like to do about that?

Those later inferences should lead you to a conclusion, a way of understanding the text that you feel comfortable with.

The step from making inferences to drawing a conclusion is small. Once you make the big leap to inference, you simply give your inferences some additional thought. You look back at the details of the text, you reconsider the connections and relationships you established earlier to see if they are still tenable. And you see if additional details support your inferences.

To illustrate how to draw a conclusion, let's return to Frost's "The Span of Life." After collecting our observations and inferences, we can decide that Frost's poem is about growing old, mostly about the aging of human beings (though the aging of dogs is included as well). We can say this because the poem emphasizes the act of remembering, a human act that encompasses the dog's span of life as the human speaker understands it. The span of the dog's life is vividly suggested in the way an image of the young pup flashes across the speaker's mind as he watches the old dog's backward barking movement. The poet need not make explicit the connection between the speaker and his dog. In fact, poetic texts often work by just this kind of suggestion and implication. They don't tell us readers explicitly what they might mean. Instead they allow us to decide about those meanings for ourselves.

Our interpretation of Frost's little poem represents one way to read it. We will remain satisfied that even though our understanding of the poem cannot be proven, it can be shared with others. By citing details of the poem as evidence to support our claims about it (that it is, in fact, a poem) and about its meaning (that it s not primarily about dogs), we can make a persuasive case. We can thus be confident that our interpretation makes sense not only to ourselves but to other readers as well.

Chapter 9

Developing Thinking Skills

Chapter Highlights

Different kinds of thinking serve different purposes and produce different results. Usually we identify thinking with logic and reasoning. But creative thinking is equally important. This chapter will focus on various strategies for improving your ability to think creatively. Topics covered include:

- Comparing different types of thinking
- Using the techniques of creative thinking
- Overcoming obstacles to thinking

Key Questions

1. What type of thinking is the kind usually described as important by your teachers?
2. Have you ever been encouraged to think creatively? When? By whom?
3. Do you believe that creative thinking can be learned and practiced? Why or why not?
4. Do you think logic is the only or the best kind of thinking? Why or why not?

5. Who—whether they are people you know or influential individuals from history—do you consider good thinkers?
6. What are the qualities of good thinking?

Comparing Creative and Logical Thinking

Creative thinking provides an alternative to logical thinking. Since these two kinds of thinking differ in important ways, you should know their separate values and limits. Each allows you to do things you cannot do with the other. Logical thinking, for example, enables you to evaluate ideas. But to generate the ideas you are going to evaluate, you first need to use creative thinking. Here are some other ways the two kinds of thinking differ.

- *Creative thinking* puts things together, synthesizing them. *Logical thinking* analyzes things, taking them apart.
- *Creative thinking* generates new ideas. *Logical thinking* develops and evaluates ideas that have already been formulated.
- *Creative thinking* explores many alternatives; it is unconcerned with being right in every particular. *Logical thinking* focuses on finding a single answer and being right at each step of the way.
- *Creative thinking* is inclusive, admitting all ideas no matter how trivial or outrageous they may seem. *Logical thinking* is selective, screening out and eliminating unpromising possibilities.
- *Creative thinking* is random. Moving backward as well as forward, in circles as well as in straight lines, it permits jumps beyond the next step in a logical sequence. *Logical thinking,* on the other hand, is linear and sequential. It moves from point to point in a straight line, allowing for no skips or gaps.
- *Creative thinking* forestalls judgment, deliberately delaying critical evaluation. *Logical thinking* encourages making judgments, assessing whether an idea or piece of evidence is valid.
- *Creative thinking* is questioning, tentative, provisional. It adds the hypothetical, the *what if,* to logical thinking's *how. Logical thinking* is more assertive, confident, sure of itself.
- Creative and logical thinking both ask *why?* In *creative thinking,* the *why* stimulates further thought. In *logical thinking,* the *why* answers a question or proposes a solution to a problem.
- *Creative thinking* encourages humor and fluidity; it is unsystematic and flexible. *Logical thinking* prizes seriousness and rigor; it is systematic and methodical.

Despite their differences, creative and logical thinking complement each other. You need to think creatively to generate ideas and logically to evaluate them. Developing skill in using both types of thinking in everyday life, in school, and at work will increase your chances of success and will provide you with the pleasure of developing your intellectual abilities.

Although you can use specific techniques to think more creatively and more logically, both skills are habits of mind, not simply tricks. You need to develop and apply these mental habits consistently if they are to become useful in your academic and professional life.

Techniques of Creative Thinking

There are many ways to develop the ability to think creatively. The following are among the most helpful.

Overview of Creative Thinking Techniques

- Establish a quota of alternatives
- Reverse relationships
- Use analogy
- Shift attention
- Deny the negative
- Ask questions

Establishing a Quota of Alternatives

Usually, when you search for an alternative in making a decision or solving a problem, you do so to find the single best alternative. You may be looking for the best bargain in a computer or the most suitable companion for a date. In creative thinking, the goal is not to find the single best alternative but to generate as many alternatives as seems reasonable. One way to avoid becoming too easily satisfied with the first reasonable alternative you find is to establish a *quota of alternatives*, a set number of different possibilities. Even though you may initially find a very good solution, if you challenge yourself to find, say, four solutions, you may discover even better ones later. For instance, if you are required to select your own topic for a research paper, do not limit yourself to the first topic that comes to mind. Instead, think of three or four very different possibilities. And once you decide on a topic, avoid settling on the first approach you can think of. Consider different ways you might develop and organize the paper.

To practice applying this technique, consider the following scenario and explanation.

Each weekday morning a woman takes the elevator in her office building to the tenth floor. She gets out there and walks up to the sixteenth floor, where her office is located. After work, she enters the elevator on the sixteenth floor and rides down to the first floor. She exits and heads home.

One possible explanation for the woman's behavior is that she uses the bathroom on the tenth floor, the only floor in the building with bathrooms. Another is that she may stop there to meet a friend who works on the tenth floor.

Exercise 9-1

Think of two other explanations for the woman's elevator-riding behavior.

Exercise 9-2

Look over a paper you wrote for one of your courses. Rewrite the introduction two different ways. Begin with a quotation or with an anecdote. Or begin with a question. Do the same for the conclusion, trying various strategies such as ending with a question, quotation, or a reference to something from your opening.

Reversing Relationships

When you *reverse relationships*, you turn something around and approach it from an opposite direction. Sometimes you need to go backward before going forward. To jump over an obstacle, you take a number of steps back to get a running start to leap over it. In reading a book, instead of simply continuing where you left off, you might reread a few pages before continuing forward. In writing out your views about a controversial issue, you might begin by

---

Taking Stock

Consider a poem or short story you have read recently, perhaps one you discussed in class. Develop two separate potential interpretations of the work. Explain each interpretation in a paragraph.

arguing for one view, then change direction and argue the merits of the opposite position. This kind of mental switching will help you to understand the logic of competing arguments, an understanding that will help you counter the arguments you oppose in developing your own position.

Some less conventional reversals include thinking of the water warming the ice in a glass instead of the ice cooling the water. Instead of thinking of the legs of a table supporting its top, think of the legs as suspended from the table top. Or consider how, as Emily Dickinson has written, "Much Madness is divinest Sense . . . Much Sense—the starkest Madness."

Reversing relationships can spur you to think more creatively by allowing you to break away from fixed ways of thinking. Like setting a quota of alternatives, reversing relationships can help you generate ideas for your course assignments.

Using Analogy

Writers use *analogy,* a comparison of similar features shared by two different things, to clarify, illustrate, and explain their ideas. To clarify different generations of family relationships, for example, you might use the analogy of a tree branching from a central trunk. To illustrate how knee joints work, you might make an analogy with a hinge.

Although using analogy in building a logical argument is generally discouraged, you should feel free to use analogy in creative thinking. Analogy can help you generate ideas. Consider how falling in love can be described by analogy with magic: *He was under her spell.* Or: *She found him absolutely enchanting.* In writing an essay exploring this facet of being in love, you could build on this analogy. You could also use other analogies to describe still other ways to think about falling in love.

Analogy can help you think of things differently and can help you think about things in previously unthought of ways. Consider how the writer of the following analogy stimulates this kind of thinking.

> The secret of torture, like the secret of French cuisine, is that nothing is unthinkable. The human body is like a foodstuff, to be grilled, pounded, filleted. Every opening exists to be stuffed, all flesh to be carved off the bone. You take an ordinary wheel, a heavy wooden wheel with spokes. You lay the victim on the ground with blocks of wood at strategic points under his shoulders, legs, and arms. . . . Who would have thought to do this with a man and a wheel? But, then, who would have thought to take the disgusting snail, force it to render its ooze, stuff it in its own shell with garlic butter, bake it, and eat it?

> *Source:* Phyllis Rose, "Tools of Torture"

Exercise 9-3

Write a paragraph in which you develop an analogy of your own. If you like, you can use the analogy to illustrate a point. One suggestion: think of something you know how to do well, then explain or describe how to do it by using an analogy. Some suggestions: skiing, swimming, grilling meat, shooting a basketball, taking photographs, drawing, finding lost possessions.

Shifting Attention

Sometimes in writing you run up against a dead end or run out of ideas because you focus too sharply on a single aspect of your subject. Deliberately shifting attention away from the dominant element can lead you to additional ideas. For example, in writing a paper about the effects of excessive drinking, you may be concentrating on its effects on an individual drinker. Simply shifting to the effects of alcohol on the drinker's family and friends will stimulate further thought and additional ideas. So will a different kind of shift, one to a consideration of the broader social consequences of alcoholism. On such an occasion you might find yourself readjusting the focus of your paper, perhaps revising your initial purpose, point, and intended emphasis.

A shift of attention can lead to the solution of a problem, as this example demonstrates: As a man is driving home from work, his car comes to a halt. Lifting up the hood, he notices that he has a broken fanbelt. His solution? He takes off his necktie and ties it tightly in the fanbelt position. He drives a quarter mile to the nearest service station and replaces his fanbelt. With the money he saves on a towing charge, he buys a new tie.

Denying the Negative

In contrast to the tendency of logical thinking to reject ideas, creative thinking encourages saying "Yes, perhaps," rather than "No." Instead of thinking that something will not work, that an approach to a problem is unrealistic or inadequate, that an idea is silly or erroneous, stop yourself. Deny the negative. Be careful not to reject the idea, regardless of its degree of promise; a poor idea may lead to a better one. As you consider the limitations of one idea, something better may emerge. You may discover that a mistake you made in writing up a lab report leads you to an unintended but lucky alternative solution.

Moreover, sometimes a discovery follows from a mistaken idea. One example is Guglielmo Marconi's attempt to send a radio signal across the Atlantic. Marconi (1874–1937), an Italian physicist and inventor, worked under the assumption that the transmitted radio waves could bend and follow the curvature of the earth. Scientifically, this hypothesis was incorrect since such

Taking Stock

For part of one day, record how often you hear people using the negative to deny a prospect or possibility. Notice, too, how often you do this yourself. On at least one of those occasions, wait and consider how what is being denied may perhaps be possible after all. Or let the unpromising possibility sit for a while, and see if a better alternative emerges. Write about this experience.

waves travel in straight lines. Marconi sent the signals anyway, and they streamed into space rather than across the Atlantic, as he had expected them to. However, what neither he nor other experts knew at the time was that the upper atmosphere bounced his transmission back to the ground on the other side of the Atlantic, making communication across the ocean possible. His radio signals had been successfully transmitted after all, even though he misunderstood how the transmission actually occurred.

Asking Questions

Born inquisitive, we continue through childhood asking thousands of questions. As we grow older, we begin to be more interested in answers than in questions. This is an unfortunate shift of focus because when we are no longer asking questions, we may cease looking for better answers.

It is easy to develop a questioning attitude. Without becoming obsessive about it, you can question your parents, teachers, friends, and especially yourself. You can practice asking questions by making a game of questioning some of the assertions you encounter every day. These can come from radio and television, class lectures, reading and conversation, and your own thoughts.

The most productive kinds of questions lead to further thought. Best are open-ended questions that do not lead to a single, conclusive answer. Questions beginning with the words *why* and *how* open up thought rather than close it off. Questions that hypothesize and ask, "What if?" also stimulate thinking. Likewise, questions about questions (answering one question by asking another) can help you develop the habit of thinking.

In thinking about how you might approach a writing assignment for one of your courses, avoid deciding immediately on a topic and an approach. Instead, consider questions that provoke thinking, such as these:

- What are some possible topics you might choose?
- Why should you choose topic x rather than topic y or z?

- How can you approach the topic in a way that will satisfy the instructor's requirements? Can you approach the topic in more than one way?
- How can you best maintain your interest in the assignment to increase the likelihood that you will do a good job? (Instead of simply settling on a topic that "fits" the assignment, try to find one that also engages your interest.)
- What if you were to do something different and unusual to fulfill the assignment? Would this be permitted? What might be the advantages? The drawbacks?
- How can you make your paper interesting for the instructor to read rather than merely correct or accurate?

These general questions about approaching an assignment, of course, should be supplemented with specific questions tied closely to the particular issues, examples, facts, readings, and uses of evidence and experience you will introduce in completing the assignment. What is important, however, is to ask good questions to get the creative juices flowing.

Exercise 9-4

Use the appropriate creative thinking techniques to do the following tasks:

1. Set yourself a quota of alternatives for improving your grades, saving time, or increasing the amount of reading you do.
2. Divide each of these squares into four equal parts. Do it a different way each time.

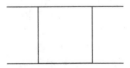

3. Describe the following figure as many different ways as you can. For example as a table, a crosswalk . . .

4. Think of two things which are normally considered opposites. Then write sentences in which you suggest a nonconventional, unorthodox view of their relationship.

    Example: truths-lies (Some truths are the basest lies, some lies the most astonishing truths.)

5. Provide three alternative solutions for each of the following problems.
   a. Shoplifting in large department stores
   b. Cheating on exams given in large lecture halls
   c. Preventing graffiti from appearing in dorm bathrooms
6. Generate ideas for writing a report on some way to improve the quality of academic life—or dorm living.
7. Develop some strategies for avoiding negative thinking.
8. Think of ways to describe people in terms of plants or animals, or to describe plants in terms of animals. Perhaps give some plants names associated with animals or vice versa. Examples: tiger lily, bear hug.

Exercise 9-5

The following stanzas come from a poem entitled "Thirteen Ways of Looking at a Blackbird," by Wallace Stevens. Add three or more of your own and retitle the poem, "X Ways of Looking at a Blackbird."

Choose the one way out of the three you like best and put it together with other ways of looking at a blackbird supplied by other members of your class to create a collaborative poem.

> Among twenty snowy mountains,
> The only moving thing
> Was the eye of the blackbird. . . .
>
> I was of three minds,
> Like a tree
> In which there are three blackbirds. . . .
>
> A man and a woman
> Are one.
> A man and a woman and a blackbird
> Are one.

Overcoming Obstacles to Creative Thinking

To become a more creative thinker, you may need to overcome various obstacles to thinking: ingrained habits, fears, even anxieties. The following chart outlines some of the major obstacles to thinking. Recognizing these blocks to thought is the first step to overcoming them. This section will provide concrete strategies to help you get past these obstacles and think more freely and creatively.

How to Overcome Obstacles to Creative Thinking

Obstacles	Ways to Overcome Obstacles
Perceptual blocks	Practice observing and noticing
Cultural blocks	Become aware of cultural perspectives
Intellectual blocks	Study—review—prepare
Emotional blocks	Conquer your fears about mistakes; learn to tolerate ambiguity
Oppositional blocks	Identify the middle ground

Overcoming Perceptual Blocks

Perceptual blocks inhibit our ability to make sense of what we are looking at. They interfere with our thinking by blocking what we can see. For example, when you first look at a painting like Pablo Picasso's *Guernica* or Salvador Dali's *The Persistence of Memory,* you may be confused by the strangeness of the images. Your initial reaction may be simply to throw your hands up in frustration. The key to getting beyond such a reaction and overcoming this perceptual block is to take a second, third, perhaps even a fourth look, to keep looking until you can begin to make at least some sense of what you are looking at. If you look patiently and attentively, you can begin to see what the artist has depicted. And you may also become disposed to think more seriously about what the work's images suggest. If you do some research on either painting, you will notice even more, because you will learn something about what the painters were attempting in these works.

Learning to see new things requires patience, effort, and practice. You have to prepare yourself to see. You have to learn to look. This is particularly important for academic work. Whether you are looking at a Renaissance sculpture or a modern painting; whether you are analyzing a social problem or identifying changes in someone's behavior; whether you are doing a lab experiment or observing qualities of style and form in Greek architecture; or whether you are learning to analyze cases in business law—you can only describe and discuss what you have noticed. One crucial element of your education is to become more observant. The more you observe, the more you will have to think and write about.

It is certainly true that to notice qualities of architectural style or to appreciate the moves of Michael Jordan you must already know something about architecture or basketball. One pillar of observation, then, is knowledge. The more you know about something, the better you are able to see what is going on.

Overcoming Cultural Blocks

Cultural blocks derive from ingrained habits of thinking that govern the minds of many people. Cultural blocks to thought may derive from your connection with particular ethnic, racial, and intellectual traditions as well as from your class and gender. For example, men and women see some things very differently, partly or even largely because of their different biological, social, and sexual experiences. Similarly, people of different religious persuasions may be committed to radically different ideas about the role of children in society or the degree of respect accorded to older people or the sick. Further cultural influences on thought include perspectives strongly tied to racial and ethnic attitudes and beliefs. While none of us is locked into a particular way of seeing and thinking because of our race, class, gender, intellectual disposition, or ethnic background, each of us must be alert for ways our culture and background may influence and possibly limit our perspective.

An example of a typical American cultural block is the tendency to elevate logical thinking over creativity. Impatience with such techniques of creative thinking as delaying judgment or denying the negative exemplify this attitude. So, too, do an impatience with error and an emphasis on being right all the time. Allied with these cultural attitudes is a lack of appreciation for the roles of play and chance in learning. Our educational institutions seem to distrust pleasure, to think that learning should be work rather than play. Play is suspect; pleasure is considered an irrelevant luxury in learning. These destructive ideas result from cultural blocks that need to be overcome.

All cultural blocks limit and inhibit thinking. Some, such as the biased attitudes of prejudice and sexism, for example, are insensitive and intellectually limiting. Consider the following example. After a car accident, a man and his son were rushed to the local hospital. As the boy was brought into the emergency room, the doctor exclaimed, "I can't treat this boy, he's my son." Since many people think of doctors as male, they block on the doctor's remark. But the doctor is a woman and the child's mother.

The first step in avoiding such inhibitions to constructive thought is to recognize and acknowledge them. The next step is to eradicate them. This takes time, persistence, and practice. It also requires vigilance. While you cannot entirely escape the limiting perspective of your culture, you can be aware of its limitations and be alert for ways to overcome them.

Overcoming Intellectual Blocks

Intellectual blocks are obstacles to knowledge. You may find yourself stuck in solving a problem because you lack information or because you have incorrect or partial information. In buying a car, for example, you can be blocked by being unaware of various cars' performance ratings, repair records, or safety features. Or you may be blocked because you have only one-sided information—that presented by sales representatives for each of the models you are considering. Or, possibly, you may simply not know enough about cars to purchase one with confidence.

On the other hand, you may know quite a bit about a particular subject but still lack the skill to express your ideas effectively. How many times have you said to yourself, "I really knew more than I wrote on that essay, test, or paper. I just couldn't get it down on paper. I couldn't organize my ideas clearly"?

To break through an intellectual block, you need either to acquire additional information or to deepen your understanding of the information you possess. For example, if you are working on a paper about dreams and you reach an impasse, it may be time to do some additional reading or to talk with someone about the subject. Sometimes an intellectual block may be less a matter of acquiring more or better information than of gaining a new perspective on that information, of deepening your understanding of its significance. If you are basing your paper on one theory about dreams, you may need to consider introducing alternative theories. Or if you have been relying on traditional psychological explanations, perhaps you should look at some medical studies. In any case, you may need to look at the information you cull from your reading in more than one way. You may need to question it and analyze it to deepen your understanding of its significance.

To overcome intellectual blocks, then, first identify whether your block is caused by a lack of information, by too much information, or by an inadequate perspective on the information. You may need to review, study, or read more to prepare yourself better.

Overcoming Emotional Blocks

Emotional blocks occur when feelings inhibit thinking. Such blocks include fears and anxieties. Very often emotional blocks combine with intellectual blocks; in fact, the distinction between them is really very minor.

Perhaps the biggest emotional block to thought is the fear of being wrong. This fear is grounded in how you think people will perceive you, especially what they might think of you if you make a mistake. As a result, you may be fearful about expressing ideas you are uncertain about. "What if I'm wrong," you wonder. "What if people think my comment is foolish?" Such blocks can inhibit your ability to speak your mind and, as a result, may impede your creativity. The solution to such a problem is to develop confidence in yourself, to allow yourself the luxury of being wrong, to realize that your primary academic goal is to learn and make intellectual progress and that making mistakes and not knowing all the answers is normal.

Another emotional block to creative thinking is the inability to tolerate ambiguity, uncertainty, or confusion. Periods of confusion and uncertainty are often necessary for creative breakthroughs. You should be aware that you may have to create or at least tolerate chaos before eliciting order from it. In writing a paper you should not expect simply to think of a thesis, make a neat outline of your organizational plan, develop your ideas, and then write a perfect essay in a single try. Instead, you should understand that a period of confusion, of trying out different ideas, of experimenting with different approaches to the subjects, and of writing some messy drafts is common, for professional writers as well as for students.

To think creatively, you have to overcome your aversion to whatever inhibits your thought. You have to tolerate ambiguity, and you have to overcome the fear of being wrong. Few successful thinkers or writers get anything right the first time. Writers, scientists, artists, and creative people in all fields reconsider their work in the process of revising it.

Avoiding Oppositional Blocks

An *oppositional block* involves seeing things in terms of opposites, such as "us" and "them," thereby oversimplifying a situation. Oppositional blocks result from polarizing, or setting up mutually exclusive categories without providing a middle ground between them. Polarized categories, like those in the following list, inhibit creative thinking.

yes/no	friend/enemy
right/wrong	win/lose
true/false	intelligent/stupid
now/never	freedom/tyranny

Do not be limited by such polarized categories. Look instead for the middle ground between opposite poles. To do that, you should establish a continuum that permits gradations between opposing perspectives. Think, for example, of being told that if you are not *for* someone, you are *against* him or her. Consider how such a forced choice often unfairly misrepresents the complexity of your feelings about a person or an issue. You may want to say, "Wait a minute. I am for you in this or that way, but I disagree with what you are doing in this instance." For example, you may favor curtailing health care costs, but that does not necessarily mean that you support the president's plan for health care reform. Conversely, to oppose his plan does not mean you are against keeping health care costs in check. You need not be completely for or completely against a particular viewpoint or proposal. Often, your agreement or disagreement will represent one or another gradation or shade of conviction.

You can also see the complexity of problems and issues by introducing the notion of degree. Asking, "To what extent?" or "To what degree?" is more productive than seeing a situation as all or nothing. Asking yourself *to what extent* an idea is challenging, a book is interesting, a film is entertaining is more fruitful than seeing the idea as *completely* challenging or not, the book as *absolutely* interesting or not, the film *totally* entertaining or not. Considering degree or extent pushes you to consider gradations and to make distinctions. It helps you explore and think about possibilities and ultimately to be both a more critical thinker and a more creative one.

You can learn creative thinking through the techniques outlined in this chapter. But because we are all creatures of habit who become accustomed to familiar ways of thinking and acting, thinking creatively requires conscious effort and repeated practice. The exercises on pp. 148–149 and those that follow can provide some of that practice. But mostly you will need to apply the principles of creative thinking both in your everyday life and in your academic work. Take every opportunity to use the techniques of creative thinking to help you generate ideas and avoid the pitfalls of clichéd, stereotypical, and over-simplified thinking.

Exercise 9-6

Draw a continuum with one of the following sets of polarized terms at either end. Identify three or four intermediate terms that represent categories between the opposites. The first one is done for you.

1. love/hate
2. good/bad
3. proud/humble
4. heroic/cowardly
5. success/failure

love	affection	good feeling	mistrust	bad feeling	dislike	hate

---

Exercise 9-7

1. Describe a situation in which you had an opportunity to use creative thinking but did not. Or describe a situation in which you wanted to use creative thinking but could not. Explain what you might have been able to accomplish had you used creative thinking in that situation.

2. Think of something you do not do well but would like to do better—swim or ski or write, for example. Consider why you do not perform this activity as well as you would like. Then think of three things you can do to improve. Write out your analysis of the problem along with your plan for improvement.
3. Identify three reasons why your worst academic subject gives you trouble. Think of one possible emotional block you could break through and one prospective intellectual block you could eliminate. Consider how you might go about improving your performance in this subject.
4. Identify two cultural blocks to understanding that, if removed, would promote tolerance, improve social relationships, or enhance the academic environment at your school.

Chapter *10*

Becoming Familiar with Your College Library

Chapter Highlights

The library at your college or university is its single most valuable academic resource. During your first few days or weeks on campus, you should become familiar with your library's layout so you know how to find the books and articles you'll need to do research for your courses.

This chapter describes the general purposes of a college library and includes information about the following:

- Using book cataloguing systems
- Finding books when you know titles, authors, or subject areas
- Finding periodical articles by using periodical indexes
- Using microfilm and microfiche readers
- Getting help from the library's staff

Key Questions

1. How many libraries does your university have? Are they located on one campus or on multiple campuses?
2. Have you used any of your university's libraries? Do you know your way around your school's major research library?
3. Have you consulted reference works in your library? Have you withdrawn books that circulate? Have you read a recent periodical article?

4. Have you used the on-line catalog or the card catalogue? Have you used any of the indexes to periodical literature, either in bound volumes or in a computer database?

5. Do any of your courses include a library orientation? Or is such an orientation part of your school's general orientation for new students?

6. What services do your college or university libraries provide?

The Library as a Repository of Information

In your college library you will find answers to every kind of question imaginable—and to many questions you probably never thought about asking. When you have a research assignment in an introductory course, the library can assist in conducting your research. When you are presented with a problem or a puzzle that is difficult to solve, your college library will contain resources that will assist in its resolution.

Knowing that information is accumulated and stored in the library, however, is not enough. You need to know how to access that information efficiently and effectively. Because a typical college or university library stores so much information, it may prove daunting for a new student to know where to begin to acquire the information he or she needs. Be aware first of all that the resources of your college or university library extend even beyond its holdings, however vast they may be. In this age of spectacular communications, libraries are able to communicate with one another and to share their resources to the ultimate benefit of all users.

One way to get to know your library is through its staff. Take the opportunity to speak with one or more members of your library staff. Ask them for their help in gaining familiarity with their library's (and your library's) resources. They will be only too happy to assist you. Another way to gain access to a large university library is to speak with older, more experienced students who have used the library's resources. Although some instructors take time to acquaint their students with library holdings in their disciplines, many assume that students can learn to use the library on their own. You can do this, but it's more efficient and often more effective to learn from others—including both experienced users such as older students and the library's expert staff.

The Library as a General Resource

Students often think of the library as a forbidding and anonymous place, a place you go to only when you have to. But besides being a storehouse of information absolutely essential for solving problems and conducting research, the library is also a wonderful place to read and relax.

You can find a comfortable place to read the daily paper, your favorite magazines, and the most current periodicals in every field imaginable for courses you are taking and for others you are not.

The library is also a great place to study, especially on nights when your residence hall is hosting a party or your roommates have finished their own work. The library can be your refuge.

Don't overlook the library as a place to go beyond the strict requirements of your courses. Often your instructors will pass out recommended reading lists or will mention in their lectures interesting books and articles that have influenced their thinking about the courses they teach or the research they conduct. You can almost always find these references in your university library. When you cannot, you can order them through interlibrary loan.

In addition, you may discover that your library has a music room or a collection of videos or art slides. Your library may sponsor a lecture series or a film series, or poetry readings or lectures on contemporary political issues. Keep your eyes and ears open for events and occasions your library is associated with. You won't be disappointed.

Library Book Classification Systems

Many courses will require you to consult books beyond those required for purchase at the campus bookstore. Often these books will be necessary for research papers, but they will also be useful simply to provide alternative perspectives to those given in the required course readings and texts. Although a library is more than a collection of books, let's begin by reviewing how the library's books are catalogued and how you can gain access to them.

Your college library, like your high school and local public library, catalogues books by classifying them into categories. Each category or type of book is given a particular series of numbers, letters, or both. The Dewey Decimal System uses numbers; the Library of Congress Classification uses a combination of letters and numbers, with letters taking precedence. Each letter in the Library of Congress system indicates a general subject area: B indicates works of philosophy, C and D historical works, P literature, and so on. In the Dewey Decimal system each group of numbers performs the same function: 100–199 indicates works of philosophy; 200–299 covers religion; 800–899 is literature, for example. College libraries typically use the Library of Congress classification system. Here is a sample listing.

BF 469 H3 [The book's call number]
Hall, Edward T. 1914 [The author and his year of birth]
The hidden dimension [The book's title]
Garden City, N.Y., Doubleday, 1966 [Publication information: city, state,
                          publisher, and year of publication]

xii, 201 p. [There are 12 prefatory pages and 201 regular pages.]
illus. Bibliography [It contains illustrations and a bibliography.]

Finding Books

To find books in your college library, you need to know two things. First, you have to find out how to access the books. Second, you need to locate the books themselves.

Your books will be catalogued in a computerized catalogue accessed through on-line database computerized technology. You can access books in these ways: by *title* (if you know it); by *author* (if you know it); and by *subject* (if you are searching to see what books your library has on a particular subject).

Accessing Books Using the Library Catalogue

The first thing you should know in using an on-line library catalogue is whether or not it is integrated. An *integrated catalogue* combines the author, title, and subject information in a single catalogue system arranged alphabetically. The alternative filing system typically separates the index in two or three parts: one part for subjects, a second for authors and titles, and sometimes a third just for titles. The most common system, however—and the most efficient—is the integrated catalogue.

Here are sample listings from an integrated catalogue.

Author listing

PS 3515   Lawrence, Frank M. *Hemingway and the Movies.*
E37 Z689   Jackson: University Press of Mississippi. © 1981.
           xix, 329 p.: ill; 24 cm.

Title listing

PS 3515   *Hemingway and the Movies.* Frank M. Lawrence.
E37 Z689   Jackson: University Press of Mississippi. © 1981.
           xix, 329 p.: ill; 24 cm.

Subject listing

PS 3515   Hemingway, Ernest. *Hemingway and the Movies.*
E37 Z689   Frank M. Lawrence. Jackson: University Press of
           Mississippi. © 1981.
           xix, 329 p.: ill; 24 cm.

Notice that all are listings for the same book: *Hemingway and the Movies,* by Frank M. Lawrence. The first listing, an author reference, will be found alphabetized according to the first letters of the author's last name. The second listing, by title, can be found alphabetized according to the words and letters of the book's title. And the third listing, by subject, is found similarly alphabetized in a section of the on-line catalogue devoted to Ernest Hemingway as a subject. This and other subject listings for Hemingway (or any writer) will be found alphabetized according to the author's *last* name.

It is important, however, to distinguish Hemingway as a subject from Hemingway as an author. When you pop up "Hemingway" in the on-line catalogue, you will find first listings for books that Ernest Hemingway wrote. His works will be listed alphabetically beginning with *Across the River and Into the Trees* and ending with *Winner Take Nothing* (if your library possesses those books). Following the computer listings for books Hemingway wrote will be listings for books written *about* Hemingway. In this group of subject listings, also alphabetically arranged, you will find books such as *Hemingway and the Movies*, *The Hemingway Hero*, and *The Hemingway Women*.

Accessing Books Using On-Line Computerized Databases

Although most computerized data catalogues include instructions for self-tutoring, you can and should find someone to show you how to operate the system. One way to acquire this instruction is to sign up for a library tutorial. Another is to ask a friend or library staff member to show you how to get started. The most important thing is to try to use the system as early in the term as possible. Computerized databases will speed your search for books (and often for articles as well). Such systems are fairly easy to use. And they provide enormous amounts of information quickly and easily.

One of the first things you should ask is what the on-line system includes. Does it include all the books in your school library? Only those acquired before or after a certain date? This is especially important for finding periodicals, magazines, journals, and newspapers published periodically—monthly, weekly, annually, and so on. You need to know both what is in the system and what is not.

Taking Stock

Does your library's on-line system include books from other university libraries as well as those located in the building in which the system itself is located? Does your library include periodicals as well as books? If so, are the articles from popular magazines and scholarly journals catalogued available for you to read? How can you gain access to them? Find out by visiting your library and asking the librarians who staff it.

Searching for Ernest Hemingway

Let's say you want to look up Ernest Hemingway. You will need to indicate by a specific system command (punching the *S* key on your computer keyboard, for example) if you want to search for titles about Hemingway as a subject, including books in which the word "Hemingway" appears as part of the title. To search for Hemingway's works, you would punch another key (the *A* key, perhaps) to tell the system you want to conduct a search for an author. Once you tell the system how to search, it will present you with a list of categories. Here, for example, is what part of one university library on-line catalogue lists for Hemingway as author. The first and last eight entries of the seventy-nine books included among the university's holdings are listed.

```
Hemingway, Ernest:
 1. 88 Poems
 2. Across the River and into the Trees
 3. Across the River and into the Trees
 4. By-line
 5. The Collected Stories
 6. Complete Short Stories
 7. Correspondence
 8. The Dangerous Summer

72. The Sun Also Rises
73. Three Novels
74. To Have and Have Not
75. To Have and Have Not
76. To Have and Have Not
77. Winner Take Nothing
78. Winner Take Nothing
79. Winner Take Nothing
```

(The repeated titles at numbers 2–3, 74–76, and 77–79 reflect holdings among the university's different campus libraries.)

Notice that if the library has numerous books on a subject or by an author, it organizes these books into categories. So to begin to see actual titles on the screen, you need to perform one additional step. You need to look over the list of numbered categories and then tell the computer which category to display.

Suppose you wish to look up Hemingway as a subject to see what has been written about him. Here is what could appear in an on-line catalogue:

1. Hemingway, Ernest 1898		1 entry
2. Hemingway, Ernest 1899-1961		52 entries
3. Hemingway, Ernest 1899-1961	Appreciation	1 entry
4. Hemingway, Ernest 1899-1961	Appreciation—Germany	1 entry
5. Hemingway, Ernest 1899-1961	Bibliography	10 entries
6. Hemingway, Ernest 1899-1961	Biography	12 entries
7. Hemingway, Ernest 1899-1961	Juvenile letters	1 entry
8. Hemingway, Ernest 1899-1961	Biography—Marriage	3 entries

Notice that category 2 includes 52 items. Since the category has no heading, to find out the kinds of books included within it, you would have to press 2 and scan through the listings. We will look at the shorter list for category 8, Biography—Marriage. Here are the books that appear on the screen when you press 8:

1. Along with Youth:	
Hemingway: The Early Years	Griffin, Peter
2. Hadley	Diliberto, Gioia
3. How It Was	Hemingway, Mary Welsh

To view the information, including call number of these books and the location and other information, you would simply press the appropriate number.

This system is logical and systematic in its approach to organizing information. If your library's system operates a bit differently, don't worry about it. Learning to use it—learning which buttons to push—will be easy. It just takes a little practice.

Exercise 10-1

Use your library's on-line catalogue to search for a subject, an author, and a title. If your library does not have the subject, author, or title you choose, search for another.

But let's look a bit more closely at what else the on-line system provides. Here is the information displayed for *Hemingway and the Movies* as it appears on a university's on-line catalogue screen:

Author:	Lawrence, Frank M.
Title:	Ernest Hemingway and the Movies.
Publ Info.	Jackson: University Press of Mississippi. Ò 1981

```
Description        xix, 329 p.: ill; 24 cm.
Notes              Originally presented as the author's thesis,
                   University of Pennsylvania.
Bibliog.           Includes bibliographical references, filmographies,
                   and index.
Notes              ($20.00) 4-83
Subjects           Hemingway, Ernest (1899-1961)—film adaptations.
Location           Hayes stacks Call No.
Call number        PS 3515.E37 Z689 1981.
```

Notice that the system lists the book's title, author, publisher, place of publication, number of pages, whether the book includes illustrations, its publication date, whether it includes a bibliography, and so on.

Notice, too, how the system lists the book's location. The book is included in the holdings of the university's Hayes Library, but not in any of its other libraries. The catalogues of large university library systems provide you with information revealing how many copies of the book the library owns and where they can be found.

What else do you notice about the listing for *Hemingway and the Movies*? What additional information are you given about the book?

These things:

- It contains a bibliography, a filmography (a list of films based on Hemingway's works), and an index.
- It was presented as the author's doctoral thesis.
- It cost $20 when purchased in 1983.
- It contains xix pages of front matter and 329 pages of text.
- It contains illustrations, and is 24 cm high.
- Its call number is PS 3515.E37 Z689.
- It can be found in the Hayes Library at Pace University.

Exercise 10-2

If you have a library book on hand, look in the front of the book to see what information is provided. Make a list similar to that for *Hemingway and the Movies*. If you don't have a book on hand, visit the library and acquire one.

Getting the Books in Your Hands

Once you have identified a book's location in a particular library and building, your next step is to locate it on the shelf. To do this, you simply need to follow the library's key or map to its storage of books. Literature will be in one section, books on mathematics, engineering, art and music in others. (They may also be in separate libraries, should your university have a large art or music program, or a school of engineering.) Whatever the situation, once you're in the building where the books you want are located, you need to find out what floor or section contains them. This is a simple enough matter. But in a large library or library system such as those found at major research universities or big state schools, you'll need to give yourself time to learn your way around. Don't be intimidated by a large library. Be patient, be persistent, be persevering. Ask students and staff for help if you can't at first find what you're looking for.

Scanning the Shelves for Books

One last piece of advice. Let's suppose you found the book you wanted. Great. Take it off the shelf and look it over to make sure it's what you expected, that it's what you really need. If not, leave it there for someone else. And while you are there, look along the shelf at the other titles. It's likely that you will find something else that will be equally useful, something you didn't notice while searching the catalogue. Scan along the shelves, browse a bit, and see what else you turn up. After all, you probably invested a good deal of time and effort to get to those stacks. Don't pass up an opportunity, accidental though it might be, to discover an unusually interesting or useful book simply because you didn't go in pursuit of it.

Closed Stacks, Reserve, and Reference Books

Some books are set aside for use only in the library proper. These are mostly reference books that are housed in the library's reference section. Here you'll find various kinds of dictionaries and encyclopedias, fact books, guides, indexes, statistical compilations, and various and sundry books containing information on every conceivable subject. Their general description as "reference" books suggests that they're the kinds of volumes useful for looking things up, books to refer to rather than books for sustained reading and study.

In some libraries you will find that you cannot enter the stacks yourself. In that case, someone else will retrieve the books for you. And, of course, you won't have the luxury of browsing and turning up an unexpected surprise by scanning the shelves. You may find that part of the library's collection is in closed stacks and part in open stacks to which you have access. You may also find that some books have been placed on reserve for use in the library only by those requesting them at the reserve desk. Moreover, there may be special requirements for using books that professors have put on closed reserve. Check with a librarian about these matters.

Taking Stock

Visit your library and locate the reference section, the reserve shelves, and the librarians who have responsibility for each. Then locate the stacks for circulating books and find out whether you have access to them or whether only librarians can retrieve books for you.

If a book is neither on closed reserve nor on the shelves, you may still be able to acquire it. If a book has been checked out and you need it for a paper or project, it can be recalled—though the recall process can take anywhere from days to months, depending on library policy and the cooperation of whoever has the book. But it is worth a try.

Seeking Help from Library Staff

A final note. One of the library's most valuable resources is its staff. More than likely, your school library will have specialists who work in various library departments such as reference and circulation. Be sure to consult these library staff members whenever you have a question. They can save you time and direct you to exactly what you are looking for. Seeking assistance from the library staff is often the most efficient way to glean information from experts who are almost always willing to help students.

Exercise 10-3

Find one or all of the books you looked up in your library's on-line catalogue system for Exercise 10-2. Retrieve at least one of them and withdraw it for browsing, reading, or study.

Exercise 10-4

See if your library provides a handout for a self-guided tour of its facilities. If such assistance is available, acquire it and take the tour.

Interlibrary Loan

When your school library does not own a book you need, the library staff may be able to borrow it from another library. An elaborate system of interlibrary loans exists, a system that includes both public and university libraries. When you borrow a book through interlibrary loan, be sure that you understand the conditions of use, particularly the time limit, which may be less than your library allows you for its own books. Be aware, too, that it may take a considerable time—weeks or months—to secure books through interlibrary loan. Thus, it's wisest to make such requests as early in your research process as possible.

Finding Periodical Articles

You can locate articles in popular magazines and scholarly journals any number of ways. First, you can find current issues of periodicals displayed in a special section, where you can peruse them in the library. Usually a handful of back issues of each periodical your library subscribes to are available for casual reading and browsing.

If you need issues of magazines or journals that are more than a few months old, you will probably need to access those periodicals either by means of the computerized database or by using one or more of the periodical indexes. The basic procedure is the same.

Periodical indexes are organized by subject rather than by author or title and cover a specific group of periodicals that are identified with their abbreviations at the front of the index or volume. There is a **Business Periodicals Index** for periodicals that includes popular magazines such as *Money* and *Business Week* as well as more scholarly journals such as *The Harvard Business Review* and the *Journal of Economic Development.* The **Social Sciences Index** provides references to articles published in periodicals pertaining to sociology, psychology, political science, economics, and other social science subject categories. The **Humanities Index** refers you to articles about literature and history, music and art and film, religion and philosophy, and other related subjects. You get the idea.

For general use there is the **Reader's Guide to Periodical Literature,** which indexes popular magazines rather than scholarly journals. For a list of the magazines indexed by the *Reader's Guide* or any of the more specialized indexes, simply glance through the preliminary pages of any issue. Look also for the list of abbreviations used by the index you are using because the entries in the various indexes all use numerous abbreviations.

Besides printed indexes such as the Reader's Guide to Periodical Literature and the Business Periodicals Index, your library will almost certainly own *microform* indexes that index many of the same periodicals and the articles they contain. Microforms are rolls of film (*microfilm*) or sheets (*microfiche*) that are designed to be read on special machines. You will probably need to ask for assistance in locating microforms and learning how to use the machines to read them.

Typically, microform indexes cover articles from magazines issued only in the past three or four years. When you need to search for older periodical articles, you will need to consult the printed bound volumes of the appropriate index as well.

Imagine that you are doing research on economic recessions. You are especially interested in the stock market crash of October 29, 1987, also known as "Black Tuesday." In the *Reader's Guide*, which indexes popular magazines such as *Time, Newsweek, Business Week, Fortune, Forbes*, and others, these are a few of the many articles you would find:

Computers amplify Black Monday. M. M. Waldrop. il *Science* 238:602–4 O 30 '87

Crash diet. W. Greider. il *Roll Stone* p138–40+ D 17–31 '87

The crash of '87: how the stock market affects you [cover story; special issue] il *Sch Update* 120:2–15 D 18 '87

The day the market crashed. R. D. Hylton. il *Black Enterp* 18:29 D '87

Déjà vu all over again. R. L. Stern. il *Forbes* 140:35–6 N 30 '87

Diary of a decision: a week in the life of Amax [A. Born's struggle to buoy his company's stock] J. R. Norman. il por *Bus Week* p118+ N 9 '87

Diary of a money manager. K. L. Fisher. il *Forbes* 140:316 N 16 '87

Discounting the cuts [budget cuts and the stock market] J. Crudele. il *N Y* 20:16 N 30 '87

Don't be rash. D. N. Dreman. il *Forbes* 140:136 D 28 '87

Down, but hardly out [fund companies and the crash] R. Simon. il *Forbes* 140:81 N 30 '87

The dreamer awakes [Reaganomics and the stock market crash] *New Repub* 197:4 N 9 '87

Easy pickings? [market crash and arbitrage stocks] A. Sloan. il *Forbes* 140:36 N 30 '87

End of the comfort factor [effect on mutual funds] N. R. Gibbs. il *Time* 130:60 N 16 '87

The end of the rich man's boom. L. Cawley. il *Nation* 245:675–6+ D 5 '87

Fancy stuff [funds with sophisticated option strategies and the market crash] W. Baldwin. il *Forbes* 140:185 N 30 '87

Fishing season? T. Jaffe. il *Forbes* 140:322 N 16 '87

Futures shock. D. Corn. *Nation* 245:509–10 N 7 '87

Global traders head for home. R. I. Kirkland, Jr. and L. Kraar. il *Fortune* 116:53–4+ D 7 '87

Gurus who called the crash—or fell on their faces. P. Finch and M. Frons. il *Bus Week* p124–6+ N 30 '87

Heading off hard times [cover story; special section] il *Newsweek* 110:24–8+ N 9 '87

Holmes a Court's fortunes are sinking Down Under. C. Debes. il por *Bus Week* p142–4 D 7 '87

And here are a few of the numerous listings from the analogous volume of the *Business Periodicals Index*:

Black Monday's ripples begin to show up. L. Nathans. il *Bus Mon* 130:79–80 D '87

Blessing in disguise: that, contends Bob Wilson, is what the crash really was [interview] pors *Barrons* 67:13+ N 2 '87

Bloody Monday didn't bloody the Tokyo Exchange much. R. Buell. *Bus Week* p82+ N 16 '87

Bloody Monday was a blessing in disguise for the Reichmanns: living post-crash dealmaking has netted the family $750 million. E. Terry and M. Maremont. *Bus Week* p56 D 21 '87

The bombs of October: from Wall Street to Hong Kong, brokers losses are mounting. J. M. Laderman and D. J. Yang. *Bus Week* p116 N 23 '87

The bright side of the crash (surge in bonds) graph *Fortune* 116:8 N 23 '87

Buddy, could ya spare a cone? [reactions to crash] L. Skenazy. *Advert Age* 58:108 N 2 '87

Builder's buyback bucks price fall. tab *ENR* 219:48MC N 12 '87

Business list big shots say all is well [stock market plunge] *Direct Mark* 50:32 N '87

Calm before a storm? W. Glasgall and others. graph *Bus Week* p30–2 D 14 '87

The causes and effects of the bear market [market crash might lead to recession, but is not 1929 all over again] I. L. Kellner. *Bankers Mon* 105:26–7 Ja '88

Economic quake leaves mark [aftershocks of Black Monday] G. W. P. Atkins, Jr. *Trusts Estates* 127:13 Ja '88

The efficient market was a good idea—and then came the crash. C. Farrell, *Bus Week* p140+ F 22 '88

Evidence proves hedging worked [portfolio insurance programs] E. J. Seff. tab *Pensions Investm Age* 16:13–14 F 8 '88

Fact-finding follows market crash. N. Robertshaw. *Pensions Investm Age* 15:4 N 2 '87

Fifth Estate feels impact of stock market plunge. il tab *Broadcasting* 113:44–7 O 26 '87

Financial jolts still resounding [in construction] R. McManamy. graphs *ENR* 219:74–5 D 17 '87

Fishing season? [survivors of crash] *Forbes* 140:322 N 16 '87

A fond farewell to the days of easy money [crash ended five-year boom in Europe] E. Cohen. graphs il *Banker* 138:19–25 Ja '88

The forum: computers and the crash. *Inst Investor* 21:8–9 D '87 supp. Financial technology forum

Futures emerging as pricing leader: SEC report details importance. B. B. Burr. graph *Pensions Investm Age* 16:33 F 22 '88

The Galbraith speculation: a venerable economist sizes up 1929 and 1987. J. Lisco. pors *Barrons* 67:8–9+ D 7 '87

To find these via the *Reader's Guide* and the *Business Periodicals Index*, however, you would have to go to the bound volume of that index for the year 1987 (or to the microfilm roll for that year). Most of the major periodical indexes are prepared either monthly or quarterly and published in paperback installments. These monthly and/or quarterly installments are then bound into an annual volume, which is published in a cloth binding. These annual volumes also appear on microforms. When searching for articles written more than a few years prior to your search, you will likely consult the bound periodical volumes. In any event, in the *Reader's Guide* volume that indexes magazine articles for 1987 you would find articles such as the ones identified above.

What do you do with this information once you have it? How do you read a periodical index entry?

Reading a Periodical Index Entry

We will look at two examples, the last entry in the group from the *Reader's Guide to Periodical Literature* and the second citation from the group of entries listed in the *Business Periodicals Index*.

Reader's Guide

Holmes a Court's fortunes are sinking Down Under. C. Debes. il por Bus Week p142–4
   D 7 '87

Explanation: Following the title of the article is the name of the author—first initial and last name. The abbreviations *il* and *por* stand respectively for illustrated and portrait. (All abbreviations and what they stand for are listed at the beginning of every volume of the *Reader's Guide.*)

   Following the abbreviations is the abbreviation of the magazine, *Business Week*. Magazine abbreviations appear at the beginning of each index volume. The brief article occupies pages 132 and 133. It appeared December 7, 1987.

Business Periodicals Index

Blessing in disguise: that, contends Bob Wilson, is what the crash really was [interview]
   pors Barrons 67:13+ N 2 '87

Explanation: This entry, like all entries in these indexes, begins with the title of the article. But notice that in this case no author is listed. The article is an interview conducted presumably by a staff member of *Barrons*, a business newspaper. It contains portraits. The piece was published in volume 67 (numbers to the left of the colon indicate volume numbers). And it begins on page 13 but continues on other pages that follow—how many we don't know since the entry doesn't indicate this. The interview appeared on November 2, 1987.

Getting Your Hands on Periodical Articles

Once you understand how to read entries like these, you are ready to follow your library's procedures for obtaining a copy of the article to read. This can be done any number of ways, depending on the manner your library holds back volumes of its periodicals. Before you do anything else, however, find out whether your library actually contains back issues of the periodicals you need. And look carefully to see that the library has the volumes bearing the particular year and volume numbers you want. Most libraries simply have a printed list of their periodical holdings with the years for the issues they have listed beside the name of the periodical. Such lists should also indicate whether the back issues are held as bound volumes or on rolls of microfilm.

   If your library has bound copies of the periodicals in question, you are in luck. Depending on whether these volumes are in open or closed stacks, you may simply be able to find the volume on the shelf and perhaps check it out. If the bound hard-copy volume does not circulate, you can either read the article in the library and take notes, or photocopy it for later reading.

Microfilm and Microfiche

Because shelf space is limited, many libraries now usually keep their back issues of periodicals on microfilm or microfiche (though some libraries keep them on computer disks as well). You will very likely find *Business Week* for December 7, 1987 (or another magazine from that year) on a roll of boxed microfilm neatly placed in a file drawer. Here, too, depending on your library's system, you may have access to it yourself or someone may find it for you. In either case, to read the article you want, you will have to place the microfilm roll in a microfilm reader, a machine whose operation you will have to learn. If you have never used a microfilm reader, you can seek assistance from another student or from a librarian. Once you find the article on the microfilm roll, you can either read it on the illuminated screen or, if your microfilm reader is equipped with a copier, copy it for later use.

Exercise 10-5

Use your library's periodical indexes or on-line system to locate three articles on one or more subjects of interest to you.

Exercise 10-6

Find one of the articles, read it, and write a one-paragraph summary of its contents.

Acquiring Articles Through Interlibrary Loan

Just as you can request to borrow books from other libraries via interlibrary loan, you can also acquire articles from journals through the same channel. To do so, however, you must provide your librarian with precise information about the exact name of the periodical, its publication date and or volume number, and the pages you need. This information, by the way, is critical at every stage of your access of periodical material. When you first copy the information from the periodical index, you must be careful to identify the periodical correctly as well as to take down volume, date, and page numbers.

Your librarian may need this to pick the right issue from closed stacks. Or you may need it to find the correct microfilm or bound volume and then the appropriate pages for reading. And finally, later, when it comes time to write your report or research paper, you will need this information for proper documentation.

Exercise 10-7

Consult one of your school's librarians and find out how to obtain a book and an article through interlibrary loan. Find out the cost per page of the article and how long it will take to receive it.

Using Your Library's Special Resources

Your college or university library will probably have other resources besides books and periodicals you may find helpful. These may include:

- *Art collections.* Here you may find drawings, paintings, photographs, and slides.
- *Audio collections.* Among items in a library's audio collection are often music CDs and tapes as well as audiocassettes of speeches, documentaries, and readings of literary works, such as stories, plays, and poems.
- *Government documents.* Such items might include pamphlets, newsletters, reports, catalogues, brochures, summaries of hearings, and other government publications.
- *Special collections.* Items in special collections include original manuscripts, rare books, memorabilia, and other unusual materials.
- *Video collections.* Your library will very likely also possess slide collections of art, filmstrips, and videocassettes.
- *CD-ROM Database.* Your library will be equipped with CD-ROM portable disks, which contain databases of information, and computers with CD-ROM players to display the information. CD-ROM databases may exist in print form as well as in electronic form.
- *On-line Database.* Library computers can also access on-line electronic databases. Unlike CD-ROM databases, on-line databases are not portable. Like CD-ROM databases, they may exist in both print and electronic forms.
- *Internet and the World Wide Web.* Your library's computers should also allow for access to the internet and the world wide web. Various kinds of

software, such as *Netscape,* allow researchers to "browse the web" for promising information.

Exercise 10-8

Find out which of these collections and resources your library has.

The Electronic Library

Although colleges and universities continue to hold printed copies of periodical indexes, much of your periodical and book searches will be conducted via computer and CD-ROM. The age of electronic information storage and retrieval has arrived, and it is critical that you learn to access your university's storehouse of information via electronic channels.

The most important guide to the new technology is your library staff, especially the reference librarians. To maximize results, you need to have specific questions for them. Let them know exactly what you are looking for, and why. Inform them about what you already have done, what you know, which equipment you are already familiar with. Then ask what else they might suggest. More than likely, they will suggest a database you are unaware of or a piece of equipment you don't know the library owns. All you have to do is ask.

Once you begin following up on their suggestions, and once you have begun to use the new technology, don't hesitate to return for additional help. Chances are, the next time around, you will ask a more specific question that can be addressed more quickly and efficiently than the first time you seek the reference librarians' assistance. You can also solicit the help of other students and faculty who are comfortable with using the latest technology. Most people will be more than happy to help you out. Don't expect them to conduct your searches; do, however, expect them to give you a few pointers. Finally, get your hands on all the printed materials your library publishes. These are invaluable, as they explain clearly and succinctly exactly what you need to know to use your library effectively.

Chapter **11**

Choosing a Major and Planning a Course of Study

Chapter Highlights

Chapter 11 expands the discussion of individual courses in Chapter 3 by considering relationships among courses. If you are unsure about a choice of major, you will find practical advice here about selecting one. The chapter advocates careful planning so that courses can be related rather than remaining as isolated islands of academic experience. Topics covered include the following:

- Assessing your interests and inclinations
- The purpose and value of a major
- The major as a field of study
- Minors and double majors
- Clustering courses
- Interdisciplinary courses
- Independent study

Key Questions

As you prepare to read this chapter, consider these questions:

1. Which subjects do you enjoy most?
2. Which subjects do you perform best in?

3. What kinds of work do you enjoy doing? Why?
4. How comfortably do you work with others?
5. How well do you work on your own?

Before Deciding on a Major

Before you decide on a major or concentration, it is helpful to think about what kinds of work you envision yourself doing after graduation. If that seems too remote from your current vantage point, consider your major interests and how they might be linked to an academic program.

Begin by considering your interests, those things you do for relaxation and enjoyment. If you love sports, you might find yourself drawn to sports psychology or sports medicine. If you love to read, a major in history or literature may be appealing. If you are a natural entrepreneur, business may be your calling, and a business major in finance or management may be a good fit for you.

Although some schools encourage students to choose their major early— as early as their first year—in many cases you can delay your decision about a major until the end of your second year of full-time study or its equivalent,

---

Taking Stock

List three or four areas that you know you do not wish to pursue.

1. _____
2. _____
3. _____
4. _____

Comment briefly about why you find these areas uninviting.

List three or four fields that might interest you.

1. _____
2. _____
3. _____
4. _____

Comment briefly about what attracts you to these fields.

or even the beginning of the third. As long as you are willing to make accommodations to ensure completing all requirements for a major, you can even prolong your final decision about your major until late in your third year.

Ideally, however, the earlier you decide on a major, the easier it will be to choose the courses you need to satisfy its requirements. This should not prevent you from sampling the curriculum and taking as much time as you need to decide on a major that feels right for you. Though it's not too early to begin thinking about a major your very first term in college, there is no reason to decide that soon. Begin the process by thinking about possibilities that hold some interest for you.

Getting Help in Learning about Majors

Take advantage of the institutional resources your school provides before you decide on a major. Talk to professors in the fields that seem promising. Set up an appointment, and prepare a few questions that reveal your interest and curiosity. Also, ask about job prospects—about what you might do with a major in biology, computer science, English, history, mathematics, and so on.

You should also visit the career services office and speak to a counselor about your occupational interests. A career services specialist can help you identify areas of strength and interest through various occupational inventories, values-clarification exercises, and planning procedures. He or she can also inform you about recent trends in various professions and careers and make knowledgeable predictions about what the job market will be like for various majors when you graduate.

Armed with information from career services and from discussions with a few professors, you will be in a good position to make an informed decision about your major. For now, use the following questions to stimulate your thinking about this important decision.

- What are your strengths? What are you good at?
- What kinds of work do you enjoy doing? Why do you find them rewarding?
- What are your basic goals in life—current and future?
- What are your most cherished values? Why is each important to you?
- Where would you like to see yourself five and ten years from now?

Choosing a Major

When you arrive at college, you may not know what your major will be. Many baccalaureate programs require you to devote your first two years to a wide range of general education subjects. Some programs also establish special requirements for first- and second-year students. Typically, these requirements involve special courses such as those for mathematics or chemistry majors that differ appreciably from the courses required for other majors (though such requirements differ from one school to another).

Business programs sometimes require first- or second-year students to take not only a specific math course, but an accounting or introductory business course as well (though this requirement varies widely among colleges and universities). One advantage of knowing your major when you arrive at college is that you can begin to satisfy not only the core or general distribution course requirements, but also any specialized requirements of the major program you select.

If you are like most first-year college students, you will not be in such a comfortable position. The vast majority of first-year students are uncertain about their major. They feel that it's enough to decide which college or university to attend, and perhaps which college or school within the university to affiliate themselves with—Business, Nursing, Computer Science, Engineering, Education, or Arts and Sciences.

Exercise 11-1

Consult your college bulletin or catalogue to find out what majors are currently available. List the majors that are most interesting to you. Of those, choose two and explain why they appeal to you. Alternatively, highlight or circle courses of interest and discuss them with an advisor.

Usually a major or concentration is organized by a specific academic department, such as History or Biology. Sometimes, however, the major may cross the boundaries of a single department. Examples includes majors in American Studies, Women's Studies, and Liberal Studies, as well as more specialized programs in biochemistry or social psychology—and many more.

The courses that satisfy a departmental or interdepartmental major typically include introductory and advanced courses, for which the introductory courses serve as prerequisites. Usually you can easily distinguish the basic courses from the advanced courses by their numbers. The simplest, and one of the most common, systems is to designate first-year courses as 100-level courses, second-year courses as 200s, third-year courses as 300s, and senior or fourth-year courses as 400s. Thus, an introductory writing course might be numbered English 101 or Communications 110, while an advanced course in contemporary literature or literary theory might be numbered 325 (or 410) and a specialized course in Writing for Advertising given a similarly high 300- or 400-level number.

Not all schools number their courses this way, however. You may find very different course numbering sequences whose logic is not immediately apparent. The important thing is to understand the significance of whatever course numbering system your school uses.

General Advice on Selecting a Major or Concentration

If you remain uncertain about which major you should declare, consider selecting a subject you enjoy or would like to know more about. If you don't choose a major with a career in mind, consider using the major as an opportunity to study a subject that interests you or to learn with teachers you respect and enjoy. Be sure also to consult the career services staff.

Besides interest and pleasure, you should also take into account at least two other factors: (1) how your major will develop your ability to read with understanding and write with confidence and competence, and (2) how the major will develop your critical and creative thinking skills. The ability to read and write, to analyze and synthesize information and data are essential for nearly all responsible jobs. Moreover, the better you can communicate your ideas in speech and writing, the more likely you will be to advance in your career.

Consider selecting a major that requires you to do considerable reading, thinking, and writing. Pick a major that will challenge you, one that will continue to interest you long after you graduate from college. A strong major can prepare you well for applied graduate programs in fields such as nursing, medicine, business, and law. It can also enable you to enjoy the benefits and pleasures of a well-developed mind.

Whatever major you select, be sure you understand its graduation requirements. This is important. Among the requirements for the major may be specific courses that can be taken only during certain terms or after prerequisites have been satisfied.

Planning Your Major with an Advisor

Once you decide on a major or concentration, the first thing to do is see an advisor. If none is available, see the department chair or an assistant. Review the college's degree and major requirements. Check the catalogue for subsequent changes to the program. Make sure that you understand completely all departmental requirements. Ask about any departmental publications that explain the major in more detail. Many departments publish handbooks for their majors, which offer useful information and helpful guidance.

If time remains during your conference with the advisor, begin to discuss an overall plan for your college coursework. Map out an annual plan and perhaps a semester-by-semester plan as well. One reason for doing this is to identify potential problems you may be unaware of (such as a professor's planned leave next year, when you planned to take his or her course). Another reason is to increase the likelihood that you will create a blend of courses that suits your interests, meets your educational needs, and offers a manageable workload.

Exercise 11-2

Map out a sequence of study for a major that interests you. Sketch out your program with general types of courses, such as math or psychology, rather than with specific courses, such as Linear Algebra or Abnormal Psychology. Be sure to allocate a sufficient number of credits to complete your degree in the timeframe you have in mind.

Changing Your Major

So far we have been concerned with the need to plan your major carefully so that you can complete its requirements in a reasonable time span, one that suits your circumstances. What happens, however, if you don't decide on your major until late in your college career? Or what happens if you switch majors?

If possible, try to maximize flexibility in your course schedule for your last few semesters. You can do this by satisfying your school's general education requirements earlier rather than later. Take required courses as early as possible, leaving room for electives and increased choice later.

Other possibilities also exist. You can take additional time to complete the requirements. This may not be advisable, however, for personal or financial reasons. You can take a heavier courseload, adding an extra course per term. You can also use summers to complete your requirements.

Consider the following scenario. You decide midway through junior year to major in Marketing in your university's school of business. If you are already in the business school and have satisfied the business school's core requirements as well as the university's core of general education courses, you should be in good shape. You will need only to satisfy the Marketing department's requirements for the major. Here is an example.

Marketing Major

> MARKETING CORE: 15 credits (MAR 200 is applied toward the Business Core)
> MAR 200 Introduction to Marketing (3)
> MAR 203 Managerial Marketing (3)
> MAR 215 Marketing Research (3)
> MAR 241 Consumer Behavior (3)
> MAR 291 Advanced Marketing Management (3)
> AREAS OF SPECIALIZATION: Students are required to choose one of the following areas of specialization. With permission of the Marketing Department Chairperson, the list of courses for each area may be adjusted to suit a student's individual needs and interests. A total of 15 credits is required for each specialization.
> AREA I: MARKETING MANAGEMENT
> AREA II: INTERNATIONAL MARKETING
> AREA III: ADVERTISING AND PROMOTION

Waiting until late in your junior year to change your major to Marketing, however, requires you to take nearly all the major requirements in a single year. This is difficult but not impossible, especially if you are able to take a couple of the courses in the summer after your junior year, or if you can take one or two more in the summer following graduation.

But even with these options you would still have to take three or perhaps four major courses each semester of your senior year, which may prove impossible because of scheduling conflicts, closed or canceled courses, and other eventualities.

Be aware, too, that many departments provide only scanty major course offerings in the summer. Often departments offer core courses and others likely to enroll sufficient numbers of students to run in the summer. Typically, these are not likely to be specialized courses in the major.

Ask early about summer schedules and course listings to assure that you plan your program sensibly and without undue surprises. Should you find yourself pressed for time with a limited number of course options, you may have one additional possible option: you may be able to take summer courses at another institution—as long as those courses fulfill the requirements at your school. It is critical, however, that you investigate the other schools' summer offerings and that you receive written assurance that specific courses taken at those schools will transfer and satisfy departmental and university requirements for the degree.

Consider this example. You would like to take either a period course or a novel course to satisfy one of those requirements for your English major. You need to do this in the summer between your junior and senior year, but your school is not offering either of those courses in the summer. Two schools where you live are offering the following courses.

AX 121 · American Literature of the Nineteenth Century
A study of major authors along with their literary and cultural influence. Writers include Poe, Hawthorne, Melville, Whitman, Dickinson, and Twain.

ENG 205   Fiction of the World
A study of narratives from around the world. Works to include narrative poems, short stories, novellas, and novels by writers from Africa, Europe, American, and Asia.

ENG 101   Introduction to Literature
Approaches to the study of the major literary genres. Critical perspectives from traditional and contemporary theory. Frequent papers.

ENG 210   American Literature I
A study of American writers from the colonial period to the early nineteenth century. The survey will include Puritan, Enlightenment, and Romantic writers in a variety of genres.

At first glance, this appears to be a good list. There are four literature courses listed, and they're all different. You need to fulfill either of two different requirements, a period course or a novel course requirement. But after looking more closely, you see that the last course, English 210, covers more than the single genre of the novel. You see that it also covers more than a single literary period. It's a survey course and will probably prove unacceptable as a substitute for your requirement.

English 101 is disqualified since it's an introductory course, whereas English 205, Fiction of the World, though it deals only with fiction, can be disqualified as well, since it does not focus either exclusively or primarily on novels. So the only real prospect is the first course, AZ 121, American Literature of the Nineteenth Century, which should satisfy the period course requirement.

But you must still be careful. First, you need assurance from the school that offers the course that it is indeed an upper-level elective for English majors and not a survey. Second, you must be assured by your own department chair or representative that the course will satisfy the requirement for your major program. To do that, you will almost certainly need to provide not only the course number but also its catalogue description to your departmental office. You may also be asked to secure a syllabus or course outline.

The important thing is not to make assumptions about the acceptability of any course offered by another institution simply from looking at its title or catalog description. Read those course descriptions critically, looking for ways they may differ from similar courses offered by your major department. Then, before enrolling, discuss with your advisor any course you wish to take.

Taking Stock

Consult your school bulletin or catalogue for policy on transferring credit for courses taken at other institutions. Can required core courses be transferred? What about courses in your major? Is there a limit to the number of courses or the number of credits accepted in transfer?

Exercise 11-3

Visit a department in which you may become a major. Ask to talk to someone about transferring major course credit from another school.

The Major As a Field of Study

Whether you major in literature or marketing, mathematics or accounting, art or engineering, you will be investigating a field of study. In selecting a major, you will enter into an intellectual discipline. While you can't hope to become an expert by fulfilling the course requirements for an undergraduate major, you can nonetheless become familiar with the more important texts and problems in the discipline. You can also become acquainted with the field's approach to inquiry and with some of its openly debated questions and issues.

One of the advantages of a major is just this opportunity to experience something of a field's range and depth. Though the place for in-depth study is graduate school, the undergraduate major may acquaint you with the kinds of advanced work done at the graduate level. You may have the opportunity to write a senior thesis, a scaled-down version of a master's thesis. And you may have the chance to talk with professors who teach graduate courses in your field.

Taking a major involves more than satisfying a set of course requirements. It offers you a chance to learn the methods of inquiry of the discipline, to debate its unsettled questions, to investigate its attendant mysteries, and to consider its relation to the worlds of life and work. Some majors more than others will prepare you to step into the working world upon graduation. Certain business majors, such as accounting, along with others in engineering and communications, provide the kinds of technical training and hands-on experience that can be translated into job opportunities. Other majors, particularly those in the arts and sciences, offer excellent preparation for graduate and professional education. Majors in biology, chemistry, English, history, and political science are often considered prime majors for future law students. In the past, biology has been the favored major for premed students, though humanities majors are now encouraged by some medical schools. For those considering graduate study in business, majors in economics, mathematics, and English are often recommended.

Double Majors

Whatever your career goal and academic interests, you might consider taking a double major. The basic reasons are these: A double major separates you from the vast majority of students who will have only one major; it increases your options for work and for graduate study; it offers you the unusual intellectual opportunity to acquaint yourself with two distinct fields of study, possibly with differing approaches to the acquisition of knowledge.

A double major, however, can be difficult to manage. The kinds of careful planning described in mapping out a program of study for a single major are compounded when scheduling courses required for two. In some schools, taking a double major may involve an additional year of study. If you are serious about a double major, talk with instructors and administrators in the relevant departments to obtain information and guidance about how best to proceed.

Because you will probably want to finish your undergraduate work in a reasonable amount of time and because a double major may be problematic, you might opt for a minor to complement your major concentrations. Minors also can provide an effective entry into potential majors, since they typically require the basic courses in the major. In taking a minor, you make a strong start on a major in that discipline. In addition, a minor can also provide the basis for graduate study. Some schools and programs permit students with a minor in a discipline to do graduate work in that field, although additional work in the discipline is often required in the first year of graduate study.

Minors

A *minor*, like a major, is a set of courses within a single discipline. A minor typically requires fewer courses than a major. Usually a minor consists of five or six courses beyond the university's general education or core requirements. Thus an economics minor might consist of five courses in addition to Economics 101, which many schools accept as one way to satisfy part of a social science requirement. The Economics department would probably insist that its minors satisfy the university general social science requirement with one or more of its introductory courses. On top of that, the department can establish perhaps a 15-credit minor, consisting of five 3-credit upper-level courses. Colleges construct minors in different ways. Generally, these minors involve taking specially designated courses, such as a course in statistical methods or one in microeconomics. You may be able to choose from among a set of electives to satisfy part of the department's requirements for the minor. Even if your school offers no official minors, you can select related courses to study a discipline, topic, or area.

Here is an example of how such minor programs might look in history and psychology. For the History minor, students must focus on an area approved by an advisor. The Psychology minor requires a basic course (PSY 100) before students can choose from among a broad range of course options.

History Minor

The minimum requirement for a History minor is 12 credits in 200-level courses in history. The minor may be earned in one of the following sequences developed in consultation with a faculty advisor:

American Studies
World Civilization
Soviet Studies
European History
Public and Applied History

Psychology Minor

PSY 100   General Psychology I (3)
15 credits from among the following
PSY 101   General Psychology II (3)
PSY 201   Psychology of Business and Industry (3)
PSY 202   Child Psychology (3)
PSY 204   Social Psychology (3)
PSY 206   Psychological Testing (3)
PSY 207   Psychology of Personality (3)
PSY 208   History and Systems of Psychology (3)
PSY 211   Physiological Psychology (3)
PSY 218   Psychological Bases for Critical Thinking (3)
PSY 220   Abnormal Psychology (3)
PSY 221   Abnormal Psychology II (3)
PSY 223   Psychology of Learning (3)
PSY 227   Psychology of Women (3)
PSY 232   Group Relations and Interviewing Techniques (3)
PSY 255   Psychological Strategies of Coping (3)
PSY 290   Contemporary Issues in Psychology (3)
PSY 291   Special Topics in Psychology (3)

Why Take a Minor?

You might be wondering whether a minor is worth the trouble. Although scheduling a minor is not nearly as complicated as scheduling a double major, you still have to plan carefully. You'll need advisors in two departments, and you'll need to learn the special vocabularies of two disciplines. The benefits, however, can be great.

Besides becoming familiar with two disciplines, and in addition to becoming more marketable when you graduate, you may also find yourself making connections between the disciplines you study. One argument for taking a minor, in fact, is to explore such connections.

An alternative to taking a minor related to your major (one from which you can explore interdisciplinary connections) is to make your minor distinctively different from your major. If you are majoring in Finance or Accounting, for example, you might consider a minor in English or Art History. If you are majoring in Religion or Psychology, you might consider a minor in Marketing or a foreign language. If you opt for the different minor, you must be careful to satisfy the requirements of the various schools from which you choose your major and minor. For example, in going outside your major in the school of arts and sciences to the business school for your minor, you must be sure to satisfy the business school's requirements.

The important thing is to consider whether you want the minor to reinforce your major or to increase the range and versatility of your academic program. In the first case, select a related minor; in the second, choose something very different.

As with your major or concentration, you need to decide whether to follow your intellectual interests or prepare yourself for a career. (If you are lucky, these will coincide.) With purposeful planning, you can balance the claims of practicality and interest. A major that prepares you for a job coupled with a minor that allows you to explore a different field of interest may provide an ideal solution. Another prospect may be to save specialized education for graduate or professional school and to select a combination of major and minor that gives you the soundest education possible in disciplines that interest you.

Taking Stock

Have you chosen a minor? Are you considering one now? Why or why not? If you were to pick a minor today, which one would you select? Why?

Exercise 11-4

Talk with someone who has taken or is taking a minor in a subject that interests you. See what you can find about its requirements, its benefits, and possible drawbacks.

Consult your college bulletin or catalogue to see what minors are available. List the requirements for one that interests you.

Clustering Courses

The rationale for academic majors and minors is that students can follow an educational program with a center of gravity, one with a clear sense of direction. One purpose of the general studies requirements for the core curriculum is to introduce you to a broad spectrum of academic disciplines. Taken together, the core curriculum and the major and minor provide the academic foundation for future learning, whether you pursue a graduate or professional degree or decide to enter the workforce.

Beyond the core and the major lies still another area of the curriculum. Depending on the number of credits required by your core curriculum and your major, you will have anywhere from a course or two to perhaps a dozen free electives. Highly specialized programs, including those requiring various forms of state certification, such as accounting, education, and nursing, allow for fewer electives than most majors in the school of arts and sciences. If you are an Accounting major in a school with a fairly elaborate university core curriculum, you may have few, if any, electives in your program. On the other hand, if you attend a university with a minimal core curriculum—say, one year's worth of courses—and if you are a History or Anthropology major, you may have as many as twenty electives. More likely than not, your prospects for elective courses will fall somewhere in between.

What should you do with your elective slots? There are two possibilities. One is to consolidate them in a minor, either in an official minor or in an unofficial concentration you create for yourself. You may have an interest in

---

Taking Stock

Consult your college bulletin to see how many, if any, elective courses you can choose to complete your degree requirements. See whether you have enough to complete a minor or a cluster of related courses.

the Renaissance, in Latin America or Africa, in music or politics, which you can pursue with your elective slots without actually taking an official minor in any of those subjects. The other option is not to concentrate your electives in a single area but to spread them around to sample various curricular offerings. For instance, take one course in architecture, another in business law. Take a couple of music courses and another pair in women's studies or economics. Devote one to child psychology and another to the history of art, sports medicine, or hotel management.

Whichever option you choose, consider what you will gain and what you will give up. As with choosing your major and deciding whether to pursue a minor, make your selection of other curricular options a deliberate choice that arises from considered thought rather than from accident or inertia.

Interdisciplinary Courses and Majors

Still another prospect to consider is interdisciplinary study. Interdisciplinary courses span a wide range of approaches. Some interdisciplinary courses are organized as surveys of different disciplines focusing on particular historical periods such as the Age of Enlightenment in the eighteenth century. These may be taught by a single instructor or by multiple instructors lecturing in their own specialties.

Another type of interdisciplinary course will be taught by two (or sometimes more) instructors who design and teach an integrated course. Examples include professors of history and literature co-teaching a course on the Civil War; a nursing professor working together with a literature professor for a course on disease and medicine in literature; a religion professor working with a professor of art history on a course in the Bible and art; a course on baseball taught by specialists focusing on areas of business and economics, law, literature, and social history—among others. The possibilities are endless.

If you are interested in interdisciplinary courses or in an interdisciplinary program of study, perhaps even as a major or minor, speak to someone from the Dean's office of your school. Find out what types of interdisciplinary possibilities exist, especially if you have an interest in creating some of your

---

Taking Stock

Consult your teachers, the head of a department you are considering as a major, and your school bulletin, and see what opportunities for interdisciplinary study are available. Find out how often courses are offered, who teaches them, and what degree requirements they satisfy.

own interdisciplinary research projects. In circumstances where no interdisciplinary program or courses exist, you may be able to design your own approximation by clustering courses that make a good academic fit—as, for example, a few related courses on ancient Greek or Roman literature, history, philosophy, or politics.

Exercise 11-5

Interview two faculty members in your school who have done interdisciplinary teaching (or two you think might be interested in the possibility of such teaching). Make a list of their comments about the experience (or of their ideas about what they might like to do).

Using Your Imagination

Create two interdisciplinary courses you would like to take. Begin by thinking of two related subjects or disciplines that interest you. Then provide a focus or topic for the course. Some examples include courses on literature and the law; on relationships between music and mathematics; on media ethics from the contrasting perspectives of communications and philosophy; on Vietnam in the twentieth century, focusing on history, politics, and literature (American and Vietnamese); on environmental issues from the standpoint of instructors from philosophy, law, literature, political science—among others. You get the idea.

Internships

Your college or university very likely offers opportunities for you to earn academic credit in conjunction with an internship that involves working full or part time for a period of one month to an entire academic term. Education majors, for example, routinely perform student teaching internships as part of their requirements toward state teaching certification. And nursing majors typically do clinical internships in hospitals and other care facilities toward satisfying part of their degree requirements.

Opportunities for other kinds of internships not required for degree programs or various forms of certification may also be available at your school. You may find, for example, that you can earn from 1 to 6 credits or more for working at a job related to your major. As an English or communications major, for example, you might be able to earn college credit for working at a local newspaper, magazine, or radio station. You might serve as an editor's assistant at a publishing house or work on catalogue copy for a supplier of audio recordings of books and other materials.

You should consult faculty in your major field, especially administrators such as the chairperson or an assistant. Visit the cooperative education office or other career services office to discuss internship possibilities in your field. Be sure also to talk with older students who have done such internships to learn about the benefit and drawbacks of their experience.

Exercise 11-6

Talk with three people about the prospect of doing an internship in your field. These can be students, faculty, or other administrative staff. List the pros and cons of this prospect based on the information they provide.

Independent Study

Independent study offers you an opportunity to work closely with a faculty member in designing, planning, and pursuing a course of study that may not be part of the regular academic program. It also offers you a chance to work intensively on a project of your own with faculty supervision and mentoring.

Independent study is made available to students only after they have completed one or more years of full-time college work. To qualify for independent study, students often are required to have achieved a particular grade point average—often a B or better. Since your school's policy and procedures for pursuing independent study will be quite specific, and since they may change, you should consult your undergraduate catalogue for details, and you should check with your department chair. Be sure that you qualify before applying, and follow all guidelines provided.

Using Your Imagination

Think of a subject area you would like to pursue, one that is not necessarily represented among the course offerings or even the academic departments and disciplines of your university. Identify a topic you would like to study with a faculty mentor. Write a brief proposal explaining what you would like to study, and why.

Chapter *12*

Continuing Your Intellectual Development

Chapter Highlights

Though it is important to get a good start academically in college, you will also need to sustain that start throughout your college career. This chapter offers advice about some things you can do to continue the academic success you achieve in your first year. It also offers advice about continuing your intellectual development after college. Topics covered include:

- Achieving literacy
- Preparing for the future
- Developing additional skills
- Using vacations productively
- Educating yourself for change
- Achieving cultural literacy

Key Questions

1. How do you understand the terms *literacy* and *cultural literacy*?
2. How can you use college to prepare for a career?
3. How can college help prepare you for continued learning and for life?
4. What additional skills would you like to have—to learn and develop?

5. How do you use your breaks from school?
6. How can you best prepare yourself to live and work in a rapidly changing world?

Achieving Academic Literacy

College teaching and learning often proceed with an implied understanding of the kinds of conventions and expectations about college work described in chapter one. Throughout your college career you will be expected to analyze and synthesize, to make distinctions and connections, to discover relationships and perceive differences. You will be expected to distinguish between opinion and judgment. In college and afterwards, you will hold opinions about all manner of things. But it is not enough simply to have opinions. Your instructors will expect you to base your opinions on careful observations—what you see and hear and perceive. They will also expect your opinions to be considered or thoughtful—if, that is, you expect others to lend them any credence. If you would like your opinions to be taken seriously by educated people, you will have to demonstrate that they are not merely opinions, but rather that evidence supports them. Opinion supported by thoughtful observation, opinion based on facts, opinion grounded in insight and flexible thinking is no longer mere opinion, but judgment. This is what will be expected of you both in your college work and, to greater degrees, in later life.

Most college instructors believe strongly that students need to stretch themselves, that they must learn to move beyond what they already know and understand to absorb new intellectual experiences. Your college professors will usually assume that you can handle their demands. They will rarely be sympathetic to your need to be strongly attracted to the subjects they teach—though many of them will do their best to share their enthusiasm for their subjects and to make those subjects interesting to you.

Whatever subjects you study in college, whatever courses you take, and whatever the approaches of the instructors who teach them, you will be successful if you can improve your ability to read, write, think, and analyze. These abilities or skills, which are essential for academic success, constitute academic literacy. College work will challenge you to operate at the highest levels of academic literacy. Look at the following model of intellectual demands as developed by Benjamin Bloom, an educational psychologist. Bloom's pyramid ranks the types of intellectual requirements you'll be expected to meet in your college courses.

Bloom's intellectual demands pyramid works like this. Each level of the pyramid represents a different kind of intellectual requirement that college courses typically make of students. The levels are arranged with the easiest

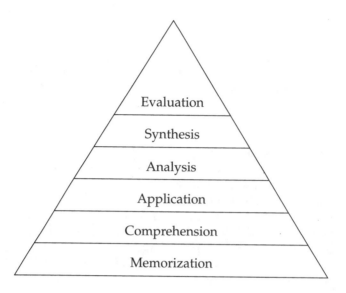

and most commonly made demands on the bottom or lowest level and the least frequently made yet most difficult demands on the top or highest level. Thus most courses will require you to demonstrate knowledge, frequently by indicating that you have retained a certain amount of information. In an introductory Italian language course, for example, you could be expected to memorize the present and past tense verb forms of the Italian verbs *avere* and *essere*. In a chemistry course, you would be expected to know and remember the symbols for each of the elements, perhaps to memorize the periodic table of elements.

Many courses will also require that you understand as well as remember or memorize certain terms, definitions, or concepts. Beyond simply giving back information, at the second level, Comprehension, you would be expected to comprehend or understand aspects of a subject. You would be expected to relate information and understand concepts important in the course. You might be expected to understand the origins of the solar system, the relationship between two mathematical equations, or the causes of the Civil War.

At the third level, Application, you can be expected to meet a somewhat tougher demand—the requirement to apply your knowledge and understanding. You may be presented with a theoretical problem, a case study in marketing or economics, and be expected to apply what you know about economic or marketing facts and theories to solve a complex problem.

The fourth level, Analysis, suggests that you can be expected to analyze texts, problems, or situations. This is a variant of the third level. Important for analysis are making observations, establishing connection among details, and formulating inferences.

Taking Stock

In which of your courses so far have you found yourself working at the higher levels of Bloom's pyramid? In which at the lower levels? What expectations do you have for intellectual challenge in courses you'll be taking next term?

The fifth level, Synthesis, may require that you develop your own hypothesis to explain a set of phenomena. Given a series of details, you may be asked to work within a particular analytical framework to select and combine a series of facts into a coherent explanation.

Finally, with Evaluation, you may have to make distinctions and judgments about what you have learned. You may be required only to distinguish between competing theories, explanations, or interpretations of a text or situation, but also to make a well-informed and carefully justified judgment for the superiority of one explanation, argument, or theory over others.

To some extent, college work involves all six levels of Bloom's hierarchy of learning skills. Most important, however, are the higher-order thinking required by levels 3 through 6: application, analysis, synthesis, and evaluation. To become truly educated, you will need to develop your ability to function competently and comfortably at these higher levels of reasoning.

Literacy and the University Community

Being literate simply means being able to read and write. The words *literate* and *literacy*, in fact, derive from the Latin word *littera*, which means "letters." Literacy, then, in its strictest and most basic sense, means being able to read and write in your native language. This involves being able to manipulate the "letters," or symbols of the alphabet, in meaningful ways.

As you know, there are degrees of proficiency in literacy as there are with most skills. Since literacy is largely a skill in understanding language, it is important that you develop your ability to use language as fully as you can. You have been doing this, of course, from infancy. And in the same ways that your ability to use language has improved as you have grown in years, so will it continue to improve—as long as you continue to read, write, and think. It is important that you take advantage of opportunities to improve your reading, writing, speaking, and listening.

At their best, college classrooms are small-scale intellectual communities, parts of the larger intellectual community of the college or university you attend. It is in these intellectual communities, large and small, that we come to understand what we know, usually through a process of negotiation with others, who may or may not share our intellectual perspective. This is so because each of us brings to our college work a particular set of cultural

---

Taking Stock

Which of your classes have provided you best with an invitation to (or initiation into) an intellectual community? Why? What happened in those classes? What can you do to foster its repetition?

---

assumptions, social attitudes, moral dispositions, and religious beliefs. To some extent these beliefs, attitudes, dispositions, and assumptions will be modified during your college years, largely through the teachers and fellow students you collaborate with in your studies. They may also be modified through the normal process of intellectual maturation and, perhaps as well, through contact with various forms of diversity.

Your part in this collaboration begins not merely or primarily with writing papers, attending class, preparing lab reports. It begins with your attitude—with your commitment and desire to increase your own level of literacy and to share what you have learned with others. To make the kind of progress in the kinds of literacy your college instructors and university administrators envision, you will need to do some reading, writing, and thinking for yourself. But you will also need to learn how to take your place in intellectual communities large and small. Even though you'll require the considered and concerned response of other literate people, including teachers and classmates, any authentic learning will occur primarily because you want it to. You learn the things that you want to learn, and you remember what you need to remember. Your attitude, thus, is crucial for developing the forms of disciplined attention critical for success in college and beyond.

Additional Kinds of Literacy

There is not one literacy; there are many literacies. The primary literacy, the one upon which the others depend, is *verbal literacy*, or an ability to read and write with confidence and competence. There is also *visual literacy*, which requires skill in making sense of what you see, whether these sightings be of great works of art or of contemporary films. *Numerical literacy*, the ability to understand numerical relationships, to analyze quantitative data and to see their relevance to scientific explanations, is sometimes referred to as *numeracy*.

These and other kinds of literacy—most kinds, in fact—require and stimulate critical and creative thinking. They require us to make judgments, solve problems, imagine alternatives. They invite our active participation in making sense of things, in understanding what we read and see and hear. Academic convention requires that we learn to be critical thinkers, challenging and questioning much of what we are told, seeking explanations and reasons for accepting what we believe as true and valuable. The academic world, moreover, also rewards creative thinking, that kind of open-minded thoughtfulness that asks not only "Why?" but also "Why not?" and "What if?" More advanced courses and requirements will demand that you know not only that something exists or occurred but why it occurred or how it came to be what it is now. They will demand that you know the difference between *knowing that* and *knowing how*, between *knowing what* and *knowing why*.

Literacy also possesses a social dimension. Literacy involves seeing relationships between your past experience as an individual and your present social environment. It involves seeing how you fit into your world as a whole person, one who thinks about his or her life in a social and cultural context. Literacy, thus, includes your sense of identity, how you see yourself in relation to others and in relation to the natural world. And, finally, it requires you to develop a familiarity with aspects of your own contemporary culture—the culture with which you are most comfortable.

Consider a recent occasion when you listened to a song, read a poem or story, watched a film, attended a concert, read a book. Can you describe what you felt? Can you explain what it was about listening to that song, reading that poem or story, watching that movie, attending that concert, or reading that book that moved you to feel what you did, that stimulated you to begin thinking? Or think, instead, of some text, a work of art, music, literature, or film that you responded to strongly—one that made you think or feel deeply. Or think of an experiment you performed or a religious ceremony you participated in. Most likely that experience, whatever it was, has become part of you. It has become what we might call an "identity touchstone," because it expresses something important to you as an individual. In some personal and powerful way, you have made that experience your own. The experience may also have provided a key to unlock your understanding of the world, other people, or yourself. Perhaps it has provided you with a standard of reference by which to judge other kinds of experience. Or perhaps it may serve as a frame through which you perceive and understand elements of your life.

Now think of some text or work that you didn't understand the first time you encountered it. Perhaps it was a painting you looked at or a poem or novel you read. Perhaps it was a song whose lyrics puzzled you or a film you couldn't make much sense of. You may have dismissed it as boring or stupid or meaningless. And perhaps, for you, at the time it was. Or perhaps you felt that there was indeed something to the work, even though you had trouble figuring out what it was. Such a questioning of your response is healthy and valuable, primarily because it starts you thinking about both the text and your reactions to it. On one hand, this questioning invites you to reflect on yourself, on why you didn't like or understand the work. On the other hand, it may lead you back to take another look, to reconsider what you saw, heard, or read.

On those occasions when you are moved by a work, when it makes a strong and meaningful impression, you begin to live with that work and let it begin to live within you. You may begin to engage in a dialogue with the work so that it may affect how you think and see and even how you live. To respond fully to a work of art, you have to invest yourself in it. You have to give it time to work on you, speak to you, engage your imagination, intellect, and feelings. When this happens, learning will have become more than a mere academic exercise. Instead, it will have become something that matters to you. And that, essentially, is what you should aim for in developing your understanding of culture high and low.

Exercise 12-1

Write a paragraph or two explaining what kinds of literacies you possess and what kinds you feel are underdeveloped. What are the identity touchstones in your life now?

Using Your Vacations Productively

If you have a full-time or part-time job, your academic vacation periods may already be accounted for. But if you have the luxury of attending school and not working, or if you can get some time off during school vacations, you may wish to consider different options for productive, educational use of your time. Normally a vacation is a time to relax and unwind. It is often necessary that we do just that on a vacation. However, a vacation period can also provide you with a chance to do some of the educational things you don't have time for during the academic term.

Another possibility to consider is applying for an internship. Your school (or your major) may have an internship program or be able to put you in contact with another program or school that offers one. Consider the advantages of an internship from the standpoint of experience, understanding of the field, and possible contacts as well as financial incentives that may be included.

There is the further possibility of studying during vacations. You can take extra courses and accelerate your progress toward your degree. Or you could do less formal study, perhaps taking noncredit courses for personal enrichment or to develop technical, interpersonal, computer, or language skills. Or you might decide simply to create your own program of independent reading, using your time to read the books you didn't have time to read while classes were in session.

Using Your Imagination

If you were completely free to decide, how would you use your next two extended vacations? Why? What activities would you engage in? What would you expect to learn?

Developing Additional Skills

While in college you should consider developing skills you may use later. You should certainly develop your keyboarding skills and other computer-related skills. They will help in your college courses—and, given the twists and turns people's lives take, you never know when you may use such skills.

Another skill you may find advantageous in the workplace is speaking another language. With the increasing globalization of business and the continued influx of immigrants from many countries to the United States, as well as enhanced opportunities for international travel, it is becoming important to understand and speak another language. College is an ideal time to study a new language or to improve your understanding of one you studied earlier.

A third type of skill is as important now as it will be for you later both in the marketplace and in your personal life: managing interpersonal relationships. Your college years will provide you with opportunities to improve your ability to get along with others, especially with those who do not share your beliefs, customs, opinions, or perspectives on experience. You don't necessarily have to take courses in interpersonal skills since college experiences such as volunteer work, athletics, internships, and most extracurricular activities will provide opportunities for you to develop them.

Finally, you should take advantage of opportunities to develop your speaking and listening, reading and writing skills. Take courses in which these skills are essential requirements. Take advantage of workshops, seminars, clubs, meetings, and activities in which you will have a chance to develop your communications skills. Regardless of what you expect to do after college, strong communications skills will be essential.

Exercise 12-2

Assess your skills in writing and speaking. Describe what you can do to strengthen them.

Cultural Literacy

To some extent, literacy requires you to broaden your sense of culture and to deepen your understanding of it. To begin with, you should avoid stereotypical misconceptions about what it means to be cultured. It does not mean that you have to become an intellectual snob. To be cultured means, instead, that you become aware of the social, intellectual, and artistic achievements of your world both past and present. These achievements include both the traditional accomplishments of "high" culture—literature and the arts as they have acquired respect and renown over the centuries, and also other nontraditional cultural phenomena such as popular music, dance, film, and other social customs and habits of various ethnic groups.

The word *culture* derives from Latin *cultura,* which, in western Europe around the year 1400, meant tilling the soil, or the place tilled. This sense is carried over in the suggestion that you become cultured by tilling the soil of your mind and heart, by developing your ability to think cogently and feel deeply about all manner of things, but especially about artistic achievements. For Americans living in the late twentieth century, that cultural history involves not only our immediate American past but the achievements of Western civilization and the cultural contributions of Asia and Africa as well. But it also involves a consideration of ways of thinking about and perceiving reality that may differ considerably from your own. Native Americans, for example, perceive the "discovery" of America rather differently than Europeans or Europeanized Americans.

Cultural literacy requires a recognition that other cultural perspectives exist as viable alternatives to your own. It requires that you recognize the validity of other ways of living, of other systems of value, of alternative ways of life. And, finally, it requires you to develop a familiarity with aspects of your own contemporary culture—the culture in which you live.

Many colleges have begun establishing requirements to ensure that the values of more than one cultural tradition are given voice in the curriculum. Thus, in both your major and your general education or core requirements, you will most likely find courses and programs that attend to previously marginalized groups such as women, African Americans, and Native Americans, or to previously neglected cultures such as those of Asia and Latin America.

To achieve cultural literacy, then, requires becoming acquainted with your own culture and with the cultures of others. It involves learning about the Western intellectual and artistic tradition and similar traditions of arts and ideas as they developed in cultures such as the Chinese and the Islamic. Cultural literacy includes, however, more than merely the monuments of high culture, though it gives those high achievements plenty of attention. It also includes consideration of the cultural conditions in which those works were created. It includes, further, many other aspects of life and thought previously considered more common and ordinary, and thus less worthy of study.

Achieving cultural literacy ultimately means knowing both a little about a lot and a lot about a little. In this respect achieving cultural literacy reflects the educational goals of your college or university. Your teachers and university administrators have created a curriculum in which you can become educated by means of knowing a little about a lot and a lot about a little. Ideally, you should be able to accomplish these worthy objectives. And ideally, along with them, you should become culturally literate in the process of becoming educated. Like so much about your college work, the responsibility for achieving cultural literacy belongs to you. Your college or university can provide opportunities and challenges that will help you achieve your goals, but the responsibility and the rewards of academic achievement are yours alone.

In a very real sense, then, we return to where we began in Chapter 1: to basic questions about what college involves and how you can make the most of your academic experience. At its best, your college experience should prepare you to live a rich intellectual, emotional, and spiritual life. Your courses should bring you pleasures of mind and heart; they should develop your powers of thinking and feeling. More than providing you with a ticket to a better job, your college experience should help you to live a better life and to live your life better. (And it should also help you develop the intellectual means to know what you mean by a better, more successful life.)

By the time you graduate, you should know not just what kind of job you might like or how much money you might make, but what kind of work you want to do, what you plan to accomplish, who you would like to become, and what you will contribute to society. In addition, by the time you graduate you should have developed disciplined habits of mind that can carry you beyond what you have learned so you can continue learning. You should be able to think about problems, analyze complex situations, make decisions, enjoy and appreciate the beauties of the natural world and the artistic creations of many peoples and cultures. You should come away from your college experience with an ability to ask and answer important questions. You should settle for nothing less than developing powers of mind that take you to the top of the intellectual demands pyramid so that you can observe and connect, analyze and synthesize, relate and distinguish, explore and evaluate, extrapolate and imagine.

When you've done that, you will have acquired the best that a truly liberal education can offer you: a free mind, a mind confident about its ability to continue learning without teachers and academic programs, a mind that has learned how to learn beyond university walls. Since you're investing your time, energy, and money, why not take the best your college or university has to offer? Why not get the most you can from your academic experience? Why not, indeed?

Epilogue: College As Preparation for the Future

While you are in college, it may seem that college is an end in itself, that college is all there is—at least if you are a full-time student without a job. Like many students today, however, you may be a part-time student with a part- or full-time job. In both cases, though, your college work prepares you for advanced academic study, for higher levels of employment, and for later life in general. As a college student, you may be preparing yourself for a job (perhaps for a promotion or a new job). You may be planning to go on to professional or graduate school.

Good grades are important to achieve these goals, but good grades are not enough. Better than having all As or Bs is learning how to read, write, and think; how to analyze and synthesize; how to criticize and create. What matters, in short, is learning how to learn.

College, moreover, should be the *beginning* of your adult education, not the end. It should be a place where your intellectual curiosity is reborn. In college you should experience the intrinsic rewards of learning, learning for the fun of it, learning for its own sake.

What does it mean to succeed in college? How do you measure success? Not by grades alone, surely, and not merely by pragmatic standards of assessment. You measure it instead by the long-range effects of the courses you take, the teachers who inspire you, the knowledge you acquire, the habits of mind you develop. Hopefully, your college experience will be one that teaches you there are more questions than answers. With luck it will be an experience that prompts you to regain the intellectual curiosity you possessed as a child and to sustain this curiosity throughout life. Above all, it should give you the confidence and the desire to continue developing your intellectual abilities.

College As Preparation for Work

Your college experience is a preparation for work. It would be a shame, however, to limit your understanding of what college can provide to only that goal-directed perspective. Sure, college should provide you with the skills to perform competently in the workplace. And of course you should expect that what you learn in college—some of it, at least—should be useful and transferable to what you wind up doing after you graduate. But try not to limit your idea of educational relevance to what is *immediately* apparent while you are in college. Sometimes what appears to be irrelevant turns out to be more relevant than something that seemed relevant when you studied it.

Consider this example.

A business student, an accounting major, completes her degree with a B+ average, a solid understanding of her field, and confidence in her ability to work with others. She lands a job working for a major corporation in a large city. After a few years on the job, she is considered for promotion. In her new and more responsible (and better-paying) position, however, accounting skills are not enough. She also has to be able to write well. Besides analyzing data and making decisions, she is expected to write performance evaluations, memoranda, reports and letters. She never was very good in her English courses, and she didn't see any need, while in college, to develop her writing skills. After all, she reasoned, "I'm an accountant."

This is not fiction. Like the example that follows, it is based on fact. A different accounting major, this time a man, performs well in school, graduates and gets a job with a major accounting firm. He writes well enough to be promoted and in fact has a responsible and highly paid position. But he has wanted to make partner and seems to have gotten stuck at the level just below. He wonders why, reasoning that since he performs well in every job category, it must be something outside or only marginally related to his job performance. He wonders whether it's because as a partner he will be socializing not only with wealthy people, many of whom are well educated, but also with people whose interests go beyond TV, sports, and other aspects of popular culture. He wonders whether if he knew more about history and politics, art and music, whether he had educated himself more broadly, he might be seen as a more promising candidate for partner.

College As Preparation for Professional Study

But college is more than simply a preparation for a career in business, the professions, the arts, or human services. College is also to some extent a preparation for future study, whether that study be formal or informal, avocational or professional.

While you are in college, you may think that your undergraduate education is the only formal education you will ever pursue. You may insist that an undergraduate degree is enough, that you'll never desire or need additional education. You may, in fact, be right. But in case you change your mind in two years or twenty, it's wise to ground yourself well in whatever discipline you study as an undergraduate. Why? Because should you return to college after earning an associate's degree, you will have an easier time if you prepared yourself well while in community college. And because if, after earning a bachelor's degree and working a while, you return for a graduate degree, you will value that undergraduate learning for its solid educational foundation. In addition, your admission to a graduate or professional program will depend on your performance in college, where you will lay the groundwork of your future.

If you are sure that you want to pursue not just further academic study, but a specific profession such as law or medicine, then it is even more imperative that you create a solid educational foundation on which to build your professional education. This is especially so if you pursue an undergraduate degree in the liberal arts, expecting to specialize later in professional school. As a law or engineering student, you will have little opportunity to enjoy the kinds of curricular freedom you have as an undergraduate. You will have little chance to read books for pleasure, to take courses that interest you regardless of their relevance to your future profession. Now is the time to explore the curriculum, to pursue your interests, all the while developing the habits of mind and the intellectual skills you'll need should you decide to continue your education.

Try to see beyond the limits of specific majors, of particular job prospects, beyond the boundaries of specialization. Consider how a physician who knows and understands people will be a better doctor than one who doesn't, how an attorney who knows history will make a more literate lawyer than one who doesn't, how a business leader who appreciates the arts can make a more interesting companion than one who knows only sports, business, or the law. If you envision yourself in a profession with opportunities to interact with people from different walks of life, people with different interests and talents, then the more you know and the better you know it, the more likely you will be to relate well to them, whether they are colleagues or clients.

As with viewing college as a preparation for work, considering college as a preparation for professional study is simply a way of encouraging you to project beyond what you can see and know now. It's a way of inviting you to imagine yourself in the future.

Using Your Imagination: Imagining Your Future

Create a scenario of yourself working in a career two or three years after you graduate. Depending on your work experience, it can be a new career or a continuation of a former or present one. Describe what you are doing, who you work for, what your responsibilities are.

Imagine what skills you'll be using. Picture yourself at work, and try to see if you're smiling, whether you're confident. Are you listening or speaking? Are you seated behind a desk or around a table—alone or with others? Are you—and the others—interested in what you are doing and saying?

College As Preparation for Life

College can also prepare you for life. Many of the challenges you face in college are mirrored by challenges you face beyond it. Just as in college you interact with people socially and intellectually, so will you outside and after college. And just as in college you develop a sense of responsibility and independence, so will you need to rely on your sense of responsibility and independence later. In college you also need to develop and maintain good work and study habits for academic success, habits necessary for success in life as well.

But there is more to it even than these fairly common notions.

For most of us, with luck, we will live to or beyond an average life span. That means we can hope to live upward of fifty years after college graduation. That's a long time. To fill your leisure time with more than watching television and being entertained, you will need to develop interests you can pursue all your life. To some extent, these can be athletic or other physical pursuits. Some of these pursuits, however, should be intellectual—pursuits of the mind that can sustain your intellectual interests and maintain your mind in working order throughout your life. We need such intellectual pursuits to ward off boredom. We need them to keep our minds alive. We need them to complement the pleasures and frustrations of the work we devote ourselves to. And we need intellectual pursuits to develop fully as human beings. College is the place to discover these interests and to nurture them.

Index

Credits